SINGER
SEWING REFERENCE LIBRARY®

Holiday Projects

COWLES
Creative Publishing, Inc.

Minnetonka, Minnesota, USA

SINGER

SEWING REFERENCE LIBRARY®

Holiday Projects

Contents

President/COO: Nino Tarantino
Executive V. P./Editor-in-Chief:
  William B. Jones

Copyright © 1997
Cowles Creative Publishing, Inc.
Formerly Cy DeCosse Incorporated
5900 Green Oak Drive
Minnetonka, Minnesota 55343
1-800-328-3895
All rights reserved
Printed in U.S.A.

HOLIDAY PROJECTS
Created by: The Editors of
Cowles Creative Publishing,
Inc., in cooperation with
the Sewing Education
Department, Singer Sewing
Company. Singer is a
trademark of The Singer
Company Limited and is
used under license.

Books available in this series:
Sewing Essentials, Sewing for the Home, Clothing Care & Repair, Sewing for Style, Sewing Specialty Fabrics, Sewing Activewear, The Perfect Fit, Timesaving Sewing, More Sewing for the Home, Tailoring, Sewing for Children, Sewing with an Overlock, 101 Sewing Secrets, Sewing Pants That Fit, Quilting by Machine, Decorative Machine Stitching, Creative Sewing Ideas, Sewing Lingerie, Sewing Projects for the Home, Sewing with Knits, More Creative Sewing Ideas, Quilt Projects by Machine, Creating Fashion Accessories, Quick & Easy Sewing Projects, Sewing for Special Occasions, Sewing for the Holidays, Quick & Easy Decorating Projects, Quilted Projects & Garments, Embellished Quilted Projects, Window Treatments, Holiday Projects

Library of Congress Cataloging-in-Publication Data
Holiday projects.
    p. cm. — (Singer sewing reference library)
  Includes index.
  ISBN 0-86573-314-7 (hc) – ISBN 0-86573-315-5 (sc)
  1. Machine sewing. 2. Holiday decorations. I. Cowles Creative
Publishing. II. Series.
TT713.H65 1997
646.2–dc21
                                      96-48294
                                         CIP

Group Executive Editor: Zoe A. Graul
Managing Editor: Elaine Johnson
Associate Creative Director: Lisa Rosenthal
Senior Art Director: Stephanie Michaud
Writer: Dawn M. Anderson
Editor: Janice Cauley
Project & Prop Stylist: Joanne Wawra
Lead Samplemaker: Carol Pilot
Sewing Staff: Arlene Dohrman, Phyllis
  Galbraith, Bridget Haugh, Valerie Hill,
  Kristi Kuhnau, Virginia Mateen,
  Michelle Skudlarek, Nancy Sundeen
Senior Technical Photo Stylist:
  Bridget Haugh
Technical Photo Stylists: Sue Jorgensen,
  Nancy Sundeen
V. P. Photography & Production: Jim Bindas
Studio Services Manager: Marcia Chambers
Photo Services Coordinator: Cheryl Neisen
Lead Photographer: Charles Nields

Contributing Photographers: Paul Najlis,
  Rebecca Schmitt
Photography Assistants: Brent Thomas,
  Greg Wallace
Publishing Production Manager: Kim Gerber
Desktop Publishing Specialist:
  Laurie Kristensen
Production Staff: Laura Hokkanen, Tom
  Hoops, Mike Schauer, Kay Wethern
Shop Supervisor: Phil Juntti
Lead Carpenter: Troy Johnson
Consultants: Sharon Englund, Ginny
  Mateen
Contributors: American Efrid, Inc.; Coats
  & Clark Inc.; Concord House, Division
  of Concord Fabrics Inc.; Conso
  Products Company; Dritz Corporation;
  Dyno Merchandise Corporation; EZ
  International; Hobbs Bonded Fiber;
  HTC-Handler Textile Corporation;

Kunin Felt, Division of Foss
Manufacturing Company; Olfa®
Products International; One and Only
Creations; Plaid Enterprises, Inc.;
Putnam Company, Inc.; Sulky of America
Separations by:
  Litho, Inc.
Printed on American paper by:
  R.R. Donnelley & Sons Co.
99 98 97 96 / 5 4 3 2 1

Smocked eggs (above), page 109.

Introduction

Make your holidays extra special with decorations and cards you sew yourself. Choose from decorating ideas for Christmas, Halloween parties, Thanksgiving entertaining, Easter celebrations, and projects for St. Patrick's Day, Valentine's Day, and more.

In the Christmas section, choose from beaded felt ornaments, basket ornaments, or yo-yo and button ornaments, and four styles of garlands. Top your tree with a Christmas angel, and make a gathered tree skirt to wrap around the trunk. To decorate the rest of your home, select from an elf to pose on the mantel, an elf-boot shaped stocking, and a Father Christmas banner. There are also a variety of cards and gift tags to make.

The Halloween section includes a Halloween wall hanging embellished with soft-edge appliqués and a witch on a stick. Also find party decorating ideas, such as ghost garlands, cards, and a spooky Halloween tree with decorations.

Halloween wall hanging (left), page 69.

Christmas elf (above), page 39.

In the Thanksgiving section, find an autumn table runner embellished with oak leaf appliqués. Or create an autumn wall arrangement from fabric gourds and colored corn arranged on a raffia braid. For more Thanksgiving ideas, choose from a scarecrow doll, a wreath, or button napkin rings.

The final section of the book contains projects for Easter and other holidays. There are an Easter basket liner, simple smocked eggs, and a clever Easter rabbit. Other projects to select from include a table runner with egg-filled baskets, an Easter tree with egg ornaments, and Easter garlands. For other holiday sewing ideas, choose from a St. Patrick's Day leprechaun, Valentine's Day cards, a May basket, and an Independence Day wall hanging. Enjoy sewing for the holidays with the variety of projects found in this book.

Autumn table runner (right), page 93.

Christmas

Beaded Felt Ornaments

Give your tree a nostalgic quality with these hand-crafted felt ornaments. Choose from three classic ornament styles, embellished with simple beaded designs, including a basic flower and leaf. Use metallic bead caps to finish the top and bottom of the ornaments. For added impact, trim the bottom bead cap with a beaded tassel.

✂ Cutting Directions

Cut ornament pieces as in step 1, below.

YOU WILL NEED

> **Felt.**
> **Assorted beads and sequins,** for embellishing.
> **Beading needle.**
> **Bead caps,** for top and bottom of ornament.
> **Beading thread.**
> **Gold cording,** for hanger.
> **Polyester fiberfill.**
> **Hot glue gun and glue sticks.**

How to Sew Beaded Felt Ornaments

1) Trace desired pattern (page 15) onto paper. Cut four pieces from felt, using pattern. Transfer dot to wrong side of each piece.

(Continued on next page)

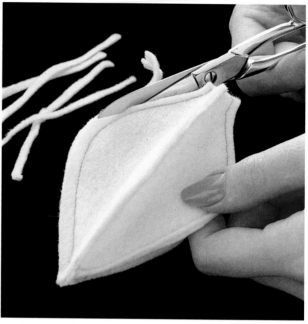

2) Pin two ornament pieces right sides together. Stitch from short, straight end to dot, ¼" (6 mm) from raw edges, using short stitch length.

3) Continue to stitch third and fourth ornament pieces to pieced unit as in step 2. Stitch remaining seams, matching dots. Trim seam allowances close to stitching. Trim point.

4) Turn ornament right side out through opening at top, using the eraser end of a pencil. Stuff firmly with polyester fiberfill, using the eraser end of a pencil.

5) Gather upper edge of ornament ⅛" (3 mm) from raw edge, using hand running stitches. Pull the gathering stitches tight, and tie knot; do not clip thread.

6) Hand-stitch through the top of ornament, from one side to the opposite side, ⅛" (3 mm) from upper edge, pulling thread tight to secure; repeat several times to gather top into the smallest area possible. Tie knot; clip thread tails.

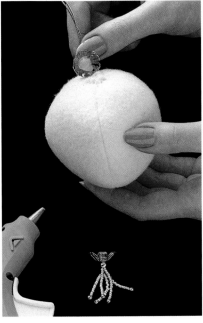

7) Adjust size of bead caps for top and bottom of ornament by spreading sides out to make larger or pinching sides in to make smaller, if necessary. Make hanger for top of ornament (below), and make tassel for bottom of ornament (page 14), if desired.

8) Apply dot of hot glue to wrong side of top bead cap. Press bead cap over top of ornament; allow to dry. Repeat for bottom bead cap.

9) Stitch beaded flowers and leaves to ornament as desired (pages 14 and 15). Stitch additional beads to ornament, if desired.

How to Make a Hanger for a Beaded Felt Ornament

Plain bead cap. Insert ends of gold cord through the bead cap from front side; then insert ends of cording through small bead. Tie knot to make hanger about 3" to 4½" (7.5 to 11.5 cm) long; trim the ends of the cording.

Bead cap topped with a bead. Fold length of cording in half; tie knot about 3" to 4½" (7.5 to 11.5 cm) from folded end. Insert cording ends through large bead; then insert through right side of bead cap. Insert the ends of cording through small bead; pull tight. Tie knot; trim ends of cording.

13

How to Make a Tassel for a Beaded Felt Ornament

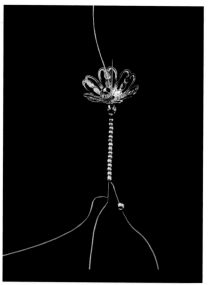

1) Thread beading needle with single strand of beading thread. Tie small bead about 2" (5 cm) from one end of thread. Insert needle through back side of bead cap to front. Thread large bead onto front of bead cap, if desired.

2) Thread desired number of beads for the tassel onto beading thread. Insert needle back through all but last tassel bead to back side of bead cap; pull tight to remove slack. Insert needle into small bead on back side of bead cap; then back through to the front of bead cap and through large bead at front, if used.

3) Continue to thread beads as in step 2; make a total of five to seven beaded lengths for the tassel. After completing final beaded length for tassel, thread needle through small bead at back of bead cap and knot together with the thread end from step 1. Trim ends.

How to Make Beaded Flowers and Leaves

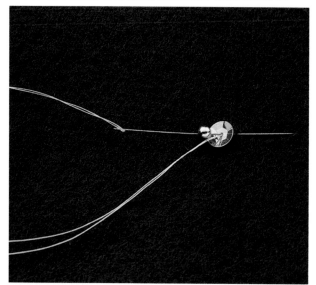

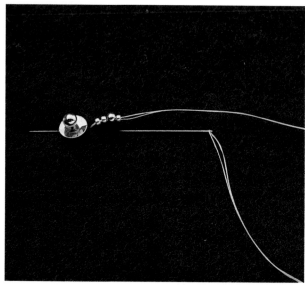

Flowers. 1) Thread beading needle; knot ends of thread together. Insert the beading needle into the ornament, pulling needle out at location of flower center; pull knot to inside. Insert a sequin onto the needle, if desired. Insert bead onto needle; then insert needle into ornament at center of flower and back out at the outer edge of center bead or sequin.

2) Insert beads for petal onto needle as desired; then insert needle into ornament as shown and back out on opposite side of center bead to make one flower petal. Repeat to make eight or nine petals around center bead. Knot thread; insert the needle into the ornament at the knot and back out about 1" (2.5 cm) away. Pull knot to inside. Clip thread tails.

Leaves. 1) Thread beading needle; knot ends of thread together. Insert beading needle into ornament and out at desired point for end of leaf, pulling knot to inside. Thread six or seven seed beads on the needle. Insert needle into ornament about ½" (1.3 cm) away and back out just to the left of first beaded row, about two beads above first bead of first row, allowing some slack in stitch.

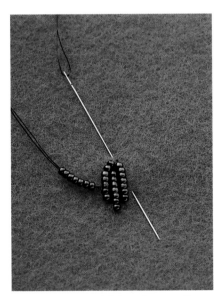

2) Stitch three additional rows of beads to the ornament as in step 1, alternating placement of rows on the right and left of first row to complete leaf. At end, knot thread; insert the needle into ornament at knot and back out about 1" (2.5 cm) away. Pull knot to inside. Clip thread tails.

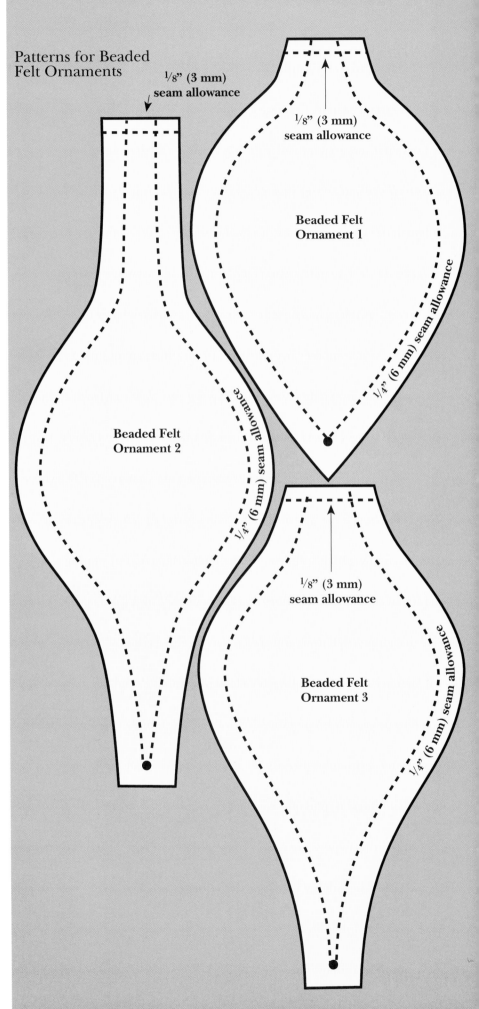

Patterns for Beaded
Felt Ornaments

⅛" (3 mm)
seam allowance

⅛" (3 mm)
seam allowance

**Beaded Felt
Ornament 1**

¼" (6 mm) seam allowance

**Beaded Felt
Ornament 2**

¼" (6 mm) seam allowance

⅛" (3 mm)
seam allowance

**Beaded Felt
Ornament 3**

¼" (6 mm) seam allowance

Basket Ornaments

Decorate your tree with elegant basket ornaments trimmed with a combination of ribbons, braid trims, and tassels, beads, or buttons. Select from two versions of the basket ornament, both made from dress-weight fabrics such as silks, satins, and brocades. One style is made from a single outer fabric. The other version is made from several pieced fabrics for a patchwork effect. The baskets can be stuffed with miniature Christmas ornaments and packages. Or they can be filled with wrapped candies. The baskets measure 6" (15 cm) high, not including the tassel or hanger.

✂ Cutting Directions

Cut one 7" (18 cm) square from outer fabric or from pieced outer fabric (page 19, steps 1 and 2) and lining fabric and two 7" (18 cm) squares from fusible interfacing. Cut one piece of heavyweight nonfusible interfacing, using pattern (page 19).

YOU WILL NEED

¼ yd. (0.25 m) outer basket fabric; or scraps of four or five fabrics, for pieced outer basket.

¼ yd. (0.25 m) lining fabric.

¼ yd. (0.25 m) fusible knit interfacing.

Scrap of heavyweight sew-in interfacing.

¼ yd. (0.25 m) each of trims, for the outer rim and inner rim of basket.

¼ yd. (0.25 m) trim, to cover seam, optional.

¼ yd. (0.25 m) ribbon or braid trim, for handle of basket.

Tassel, beads, or button, optional.

Liquid fray preventer.

Miniature ornaments, packages, or wrapped candies, to fill basket.

How to Sew a Basket Ornament

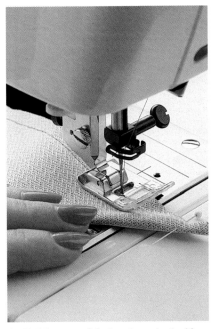

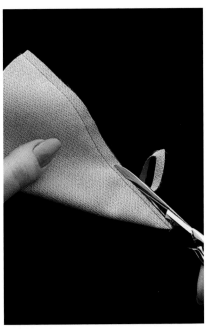

1) Trace pattern (page 19) onto paper. Apply square of fusible interfacing to wrong side of outer fabric square, following manufacturer's instructions. Pin pattern to interfaced fabric square. Cut on outer marked lines of pattern. Repeat for lining fabric.

2) Fold outer fabric piece in half, right sides together; pin. Stitch from the upper edge to point, ¼" (6 mm) from the raw edges. Repeat for the lining and heavyweight nonfusible interfacing, using ⅜" (1 cm) seam allowances.

3) Trim seam allowances close to stitching; trim point. Carefully press seam allowances to one side, using tip of iron.

(Continued on next page)

How to Sew a Basket Ornament (continued)

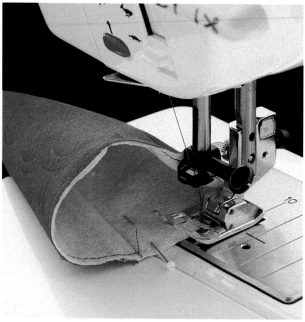

4) Turn outer fabric piece right side out. Insert heavy-weight interfacing inside outer fabric basket; align seam allowances. Baste 1/8" (3 mm) from upper edge of basket.

5) Insert lining into basket, wrong sides together; align seam allowances. Carefully push lining deep into basket, using pointed object, such as a knitting needle. Pin lining to basket along upper edge. Trim any excess lining fabric even with upper edge of the basket. Stitch lining to basket at upper edge, using a short narrow zigzag stitch.

6) Apply liquid fray preventer to ends of ribbon or trim for hanger. Pin trim to each side of basket at upper edge; hand-stitch in place. Hand-stitch trim over seamline on outside of basket, if desired. Hand-stitch or machine-stitch trim to outside and inside of basket at upper edge to conceal raw edges; apply liquid fray preventer to cut ends of trim.

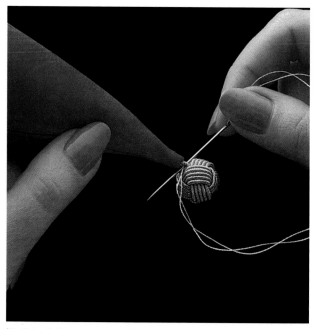

7) Stitch button, tassel, or beads to the lower edge of the basket, if desired, using thread that matches the embellishment. Fill the basket with miniature ornaments, packages, or candy.

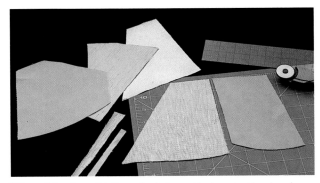 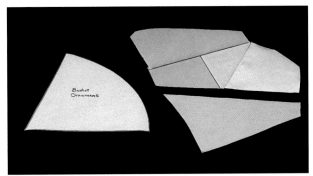

Pieced basket. 1) Fuse knit interfacing to the backs of four or five fabric scraps for pieced outer basket, following manufacturer's instructions. Cut a straight line on one side of each of two fabric scraps. Pin the fabrics right sides together, aligning straight edges. Stitch ¼" (6 mm) from raw edges. Press the seam allowances to one side.

2) Cut straight line at an angle along one side of pieced strip, and cut a straight line on a third scrap of fabric. Pin fabrics right sides together, aligning straight edges. Stitch ¼" (6 mm) from raw edges. Press seam allowances to one side. Repeat to stitch together a total of four or five fabrics as desired. Follow page 17, steps 1 to 7, using pieced fabric for outer fabric; omit reference to interfacing outer fabric square in step 1.

Pattern for Basket Ornament

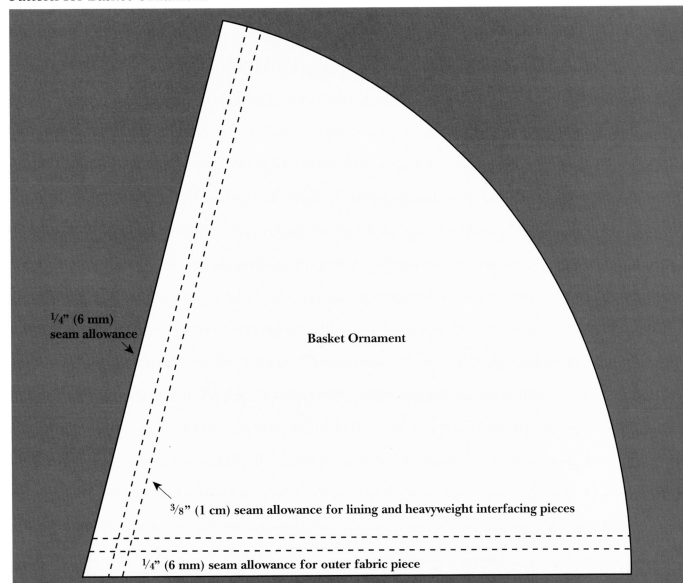

¼" (6 mm) seam allowance

Basket Ornament

³⁄8" (1 cm) seam allowance for lining and heavyweight interfacing pieces

¼" (6 mm) seam allowance for outer fabric piece

Yo-Yo & Button Ornaments

Create quick and easy country-style ornaments from fabric yo-yos, buttons, and raffia. These ornaments can be made from leftover fabric scraps and buttons, making them an inexpensive project or gift. Make the yo-yos from white or off-white fabrics for a winter effect, or use red and green fabrics for a festive look.

✂ Cutting Directions

Cut the desired number of circles from fabrics for yo-yos, cutting 3" (7.5 cm) diameter circles for 1¼" (3.2 cm) finished yo-yos and 3½" (9 cm) diameter circles for 1½" (3.8 cm) finished yo-yos.

YOU WILL NEED

Scraps of several fabrics, for yo-yos.

Four-hole buttons.

Raffia.

Large-eyed needle, that will go through holes of buttons.

How to Make a Yo-Yo and Button Ornament

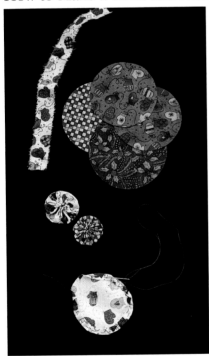

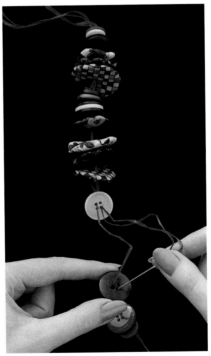

1) Turn ¼" (6 mm) on outer edge of circle for yo-yo to the wrong side, and stitch hand running stitches a scant ⅛" (3 mm) from folded edge. Pull up thread to gather circle, and tie off thread tails on the inside. Repeat with any remaining circles for yo-yos. Tear a ⅝" × 9" (1.5 × 23 cm) strip from scrap of fabric, for optional bow at top of ornament; set aside until step 3.

2) String the buttons and yo-yos as desired, inserting raffia through one hole of buttons. At the end, insert needle back through buttons and yo-yos, inserting needle through hole in button opposite previously used hole. Allow excess raffia at both ends.

3) String a second piece of raffia through remaining holes as in step 2, if additional raffia is desired. Tie knot in raffia at top of ornament, about 3" (7.5 cm) from end of loop. Push the yo-yos and buttons tight against knot. Tie second knot at opposite end of ornament, securing it tightly against last button or yo-yo. Cut raffia tails to about 3" (7.5 cm) to make tassel at bottom. Tie bow around raffia hanger at the top of ornament, if desired.

Treetop Angel

Give your holiday tree a spectacular finish with an angel tree topper. The angel shown opposite is crafted with doll-like characteristics and is designed as a holiday caroler. She features a muslin head and curly doll hair. Her coat and cape are made from velveteen and are trimmed in synthetic fur.

The wings of the angel are made from organza, but are given a shimmery effect with an overlay of gold mesh. The wings are also outlined with glitter glue. The halo is created from a circle of brass craft wire.

✄ Cutting Directions

For the head, cut two pieces from muslin as on page 24, step 2.

For the arms, cut one 2" × 11" (5 × 28 cm) rectangle from muslin.

For the coat, cut a semicircle with a 10" (25.5 cm) radius. For the sleeves, cut a circle with a 9" (23 cm) diameter. For the cape, cut a circle with a 6" (15 cm) diameter.

For the wings, cut one 9" × 12" (23 × 30.5 cm) rectangle each from gold mesh, organza, and fusible web.

For the trim on the coat and cape, cut ⅝" (1.5 cm) strips across the width of synthetic fur or fleece.

YOU WILL NEED

Poster board.

Packing tape.

⅓ **yd. (0.32 m) fabric,** for coat.

⅛ **yd. (0.15 m) synthetic fur or fleece,** for trim on coat.

¼ **yd. (0.25 m) muslin,** for head and arms.

¼ **yd. (0.25 m) organza,** for wings.

¼ **yd. (0.25 m) gold mesh,** for overlay of wings.

¼ **yd. (0.25 m) fusible web,** for wings.

Chenille stem, for arms.

One package curly doll hair.

24-gauge craft wire and 16-gauge brass wire; wire cutter.

Fine-point permanent-ink marking pen, for marking face.

Cosmetic blush; cotton swab.

Glitter glue in fine-point tube.

Thick, white craft glue.

Hot glue gun and glue sticks.

Polyester fiberfill.

How to Sew a Treetop Angel

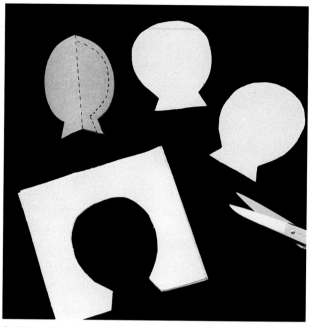

1) Cut a semicircle with 8" (20.5 cm) radius from poster board. Trim 6" (15 cm) pie-shaped wedge from one end; discard. Form a cone with base 15" (38 cm) in circumference; secure with packing tape.

2) Transfer pattern for head (page 29) to paper, placing dotted line on fold of paper. Cut two pieces from muslin.

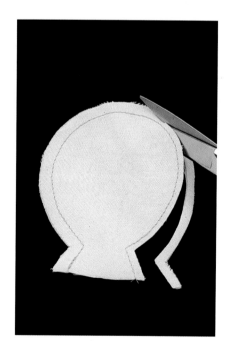

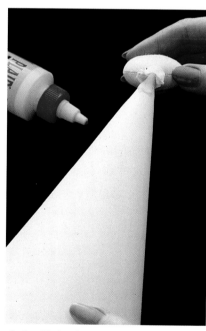

3) Place pieces for head right sides together; stitch ¼" (6 mm) from raw edges, leaving opening at base of neck. Trim seam allowance to ⅛" (3 mm). Clip corners at neck. Turn right side out; press.

4) Stuff the head with polyester fiberfill, using the eraser end of a pencil. Apply craft glue to upper ½" (1.3 cm) of cone. Glue neck over point of cone.

5) Fold semicircle for coat in half crosswise; stitch ¼" (6 mm) seam along straight edge, from curved side to a point 2" (5 cm) from fold. Press seam open.

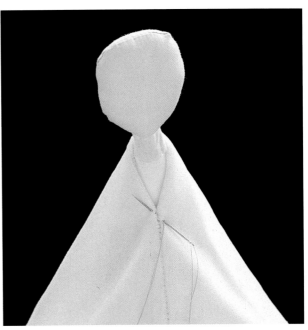

6) Position craft wire ¼" (6 mm) from lower edge of right side of coat. Set machine for a short, narrow zigzag stitch, and zigzag over wire to secure in place. A cording presser foot helps in guiding wire. Trim off excess wire with wire cutter.

7) Slip coat over cone, positioning seam at center back. Hand-stitch opening closed. Stitch coat to neck around upper edge.

8) Fold circle for the cape into quarters; trim off ¼" (6 mm) arc from folded center of fabric. Cut 2¼" (6 cm) pie-shaped wedge from circle.

9) Fold circle for sleeves in half, right sides together. Mark a point on each side of curve, 3½" (9 cm) from the fold. Mark a point at center of folded edge, 1" (2.5 cm) from the fold. Draw lines connecting points. Stitch on marked lines; trim fabric close to stitching. Turn sleeves right side out.

(Continued on next page)

10) Fold rectangle for arms in half crosswise, right sides together. Starting close to center of rectangle, stitch ¼" (6 mm) from raw edges, curving stitching to fold at end, to round one corner; repeat on the opposite side, leaving an opening at the center for turning. Trim seam allowances close to stitching. Turn right side out; press.

11) Cut chenille stem to length of the arms plus ¾" (2 cm), using wire cutter. Bend back ⅜" (1 cm) of chenille stem at each end; insert into fabric tube for arms. Stuff arms with polyester fiberfill, using the eraser end of a pencil. Slipstitch opening closed.

12) Insert and center arms into sleeves. Hand-stitch together at center. Secure fur to lower edges of the sleeves, using hot glue. Secure fur to lower edge of coat and around lower edge of cape, using hot glue.

13) Hand-stitch center of arms to back of angel, centering arms over back seam of coat. Wrap cape around neck of angel. Turn under ¼" (6 mm) on one side of center back; overlap, and hand-stitch to remaining side.

14) Glue strip of fur trim around neck of angel. Cut hair into strips, and glue to head of angel, using hot glue.

15) Mark the face as shown, using fine-point permanent-ink marking pen. Allow to dry. Apply blush, using cotton swab.

16) Cut 18" (46 cm) length of 16-gauge brass wire. Wrap wire around upper edge of a cup or glass with about 3" (7.5 cm) diameter. Twist ends together for about 1" (2.5 cm). Trim ends about ⅝" (1.5 cm) from point where twisting ends; bend ends out. Insert wire ends of halo into hair at back of head; glue in place.

17) Make wings (page 28). Take small tuck at center of wing, and hand-stitch to back of angel at center of cape, above trim.

18) Arrange the arms of the angel, and shape the wings.

How to Make the Wings of the Treetop Angel

1) Transfer partial pattern for wings (opposite) to paper, placing dotted line of pattern on fold of paper. Turn wing pattern over, and realign dotted line of pattern with fold of paper. Transfer pattern for second half of wing to paper. Do not cut out.

2) Place rectangles of organza and gold mesh wrong sides together, with fusible web positioned between the layers. Place between sheets of typing paper, and fuse, following manufacturer's directions.

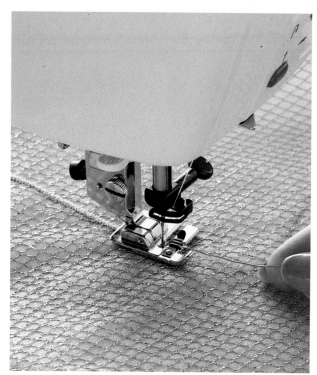

3) Pin fabric for wing, right side up, over the wing pattern. Zigzag over craft wire, following marked lines for wings, stitching through both fabric and paper; use a cording foot to help guide wire. Remove paper.

4) Cut around wire, close to stitching. Apply glitter glue to front of wing at outer edges, covering the stitching; allow to dry. Apply glitter glue to back of wing at outer edges; allow to dry.

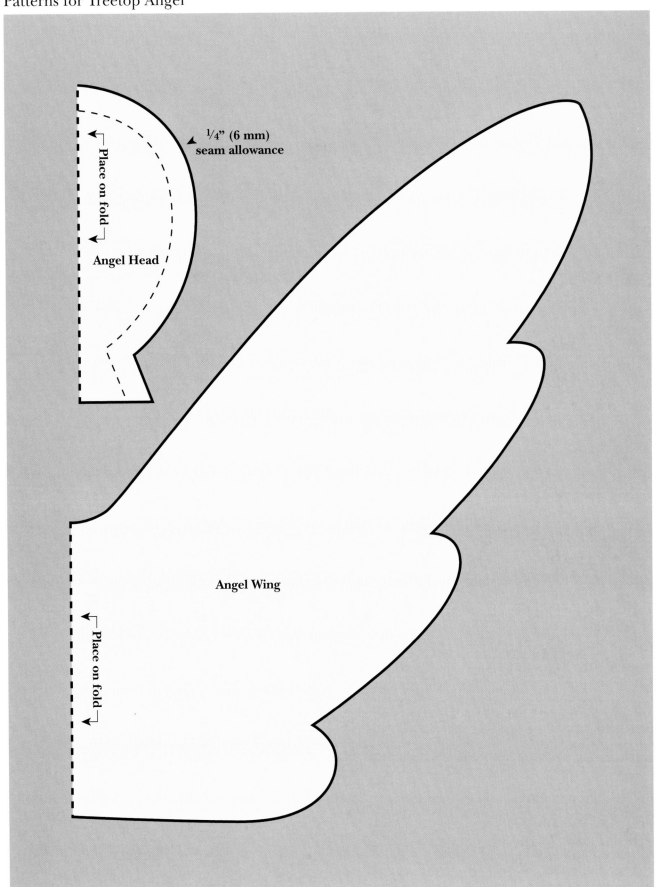

¹/₄" (6 mm) seam allowance

Place on fold

Angel Head

Angel Wing

Place on fold

Garlands

Holiday garlands can be used for more than decorating the Christmas tree. Drape them across mantels, over doorways, or across window frames. You can make garlands in a variety of styles to coordinate with your holiday decorating scheme. Shown above (top to bottom) are a soft-edge fabric-wrap and bead garland, a yo-yo and button garland, a beaded garland, and a beaded felt motif garland.

Make garlands up to 72" (183 cm) long for ease in handling. For garlands designed to be hung on trees, construct garlands with loops at each end for securing them to tree branches. End loops also work well for some draped garlands, such as those draped over mantels. The motifs used in the yo-yo and button garland and the beaded felt motif garland are created

by tracing around cookie cutters. You can enlarge or reduce cookie cutter motifs on a photocopy machine, or you can draw your own freehand holiday motifs, if desired.

✂ Cutting Directions
(for the Yo-Yo and Button Garland)

Make the cookie cutter pattern as on page 32, step 1, and cut one front piece for each desired motif. Cut one rectangle from fabric for the back and one rectangle of batting, larger than each motif.

Cut the desired number of circles for yo-yos, cutting 2½" (6.5 cm) circles for 1" (2.5 cm) finished yo-yos and 3½" (9 cm) circles for 1½" (3.8 cm) finished yo-yos.

For soft-edge fabric-wrap and bead garland:

Scraps of cotton fabric.

Beads.

Jute or twine.

Large-eyed needle; awl.

Styrofoam® holiday motifs.

⅞" (2.2 cm) Styrofoam balls.

Thick white craft glue.

For yo-yo and button garland:

Fabric, for yo-yos.

Fabric, for cookie cutter motifs.

Cookie cutters in holiday motifs.

Batting.

Pearl cotton, for hand stitching around cookie cutter motifs.

Ribbon or other embellishments as desired for cookie cutter motifs.

Buttons.

Raffia.

Large-eyed needle.

For beaded garland:

Cording.

Beads.

Tape; liquid fray preventer.

For beaded felt motif garland:

Felt, for motifs.

Cookie cutters in holiday motifs.

Polyester fiberfill.

Beads for stringing between motifs.

Decorative cording, braid, or ribbon, for stringing motifs and beads.

Embellishments, such as buttons, beads, or bells, optional.

How to Make a Soft-edge Fabric-wrap and Bead Garland

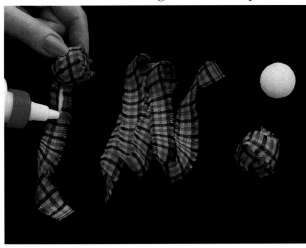

1) Tear ⅝" (1.5 cm) strips across the width of the fabrics; press. Wrap one torn fabric strip randomly around Styrofoam ball; secure with glue. Trim excess fabric. Repeat for any additional balls.

2) Wrap fabric strips around the Styrofoam motifs, wrapping in longest direction first. Secure at the beginning, end, and, if necessary, every few wraps with dot of glue. Trim excess fabric at end.

3) Insert large-eyed needle into Styrofoam motifs to start holes for stringing; enlarge holes, using an awl. Take care not to force awl, since Styrofoam may break.

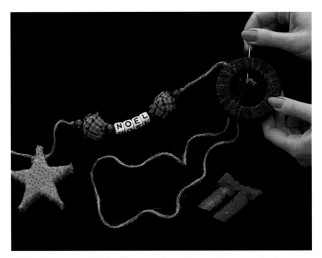

4) String motifs, balls, and beads on jute as desired, tying knots in jute at beginning and end of bead group or motif to secure in place. Form loops at ends, if desired; secure with knot. Embellish as desired.

How to Make a Yo-Yo and Button Garland

1) Trace around cookie cutter on paper to make pattern. Cut motif from fabric (above). Layer fabric for back, batting, and motif, with motif on top; pin.

2) Hand-stitch around motif about ⅛" (3 mm) from raw edges, using pearl cotton. Conceal knot at beginning and end within fabric and batting layers. Trim excess batting and backing even with outer edge of motif. Embellish cookie cutter motif as desired.

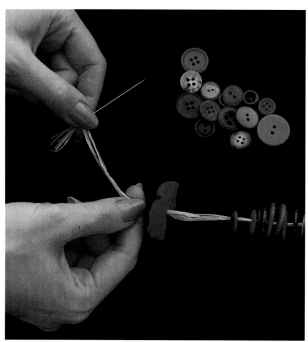

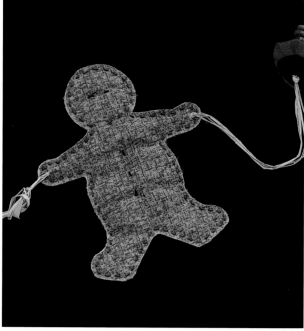

3) Make yo-yos as on page 21, step 1, omitting the reference to bow. String the buttons and yo-yos as desired, inserting raffia through one hole of buttons.

4) String the cookie cutter motifs by inserting raffia through a large-eyed needle and inserting needle through the back layer of motif ¼" (6 mm) from edge and exiting ¼" (6 mm) from edge on opposite side. Tie knots in raffia on each side of the motif and at ends of yo-yo and button groupings to secure them in place. Form loops at the ends of raffia, if desired; secure with knots.

How to Make a Beaded Garland

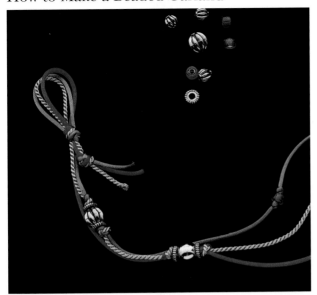

1) **Cut** three pieces of cording to desired length plus about 20" (51 cm). Knot ends together; make loop for hanging at one end. Wrap opposite ends of cords with tape to make insertion into beads easier. Knot two pieces together about 2" (5 cm) from end with loop. Insert two ends through beads; tie knot at end of beads to secure. Repeat, using one or two different strands of cording. Continue to add beads about every 2" (5 cm), using one or two different cords each time to make a length about 15" to 20" (38 to 51 cm) long.

2) **Tie** all cords together in knot. Continue to add beads to cords as in step 1, knotting all the cords together occasionally until desired length is reached. Knot ends together; make loop at end of garland as in step 1. Apply liquid fray preventer to ends, if necessary.

How to Make a Beaded Felt Motif Garland

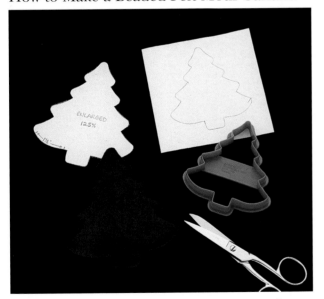

1) **Trace** around cookie cutter on paper to make pattern; cut on marked line. Place pattern on top of two layers of felt; tape in place. Stitch around outer edges of pattern, using short stitch length; leave 1½" (3.8 cm) opening on one side for turning and stuffing. Remove pattern and tape; trim close to stitching.

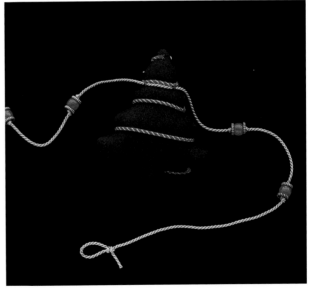

2) **Turn** felt motif right side out. Stuff with polyester fiberfill, using the eraser end of a pencil. Slipstitch the opening closed. Hand-stitch beads and other embellishments to motif as desired. String beads onto cording, braid, or ribbon, tying knots on each side of bead groupings. Secure felt motifs in place by hand-stitching cording on each side of ornament. Form loops at ends of cording, if desired; secure with knots.

Tree Skirts with Ruffled Headers

A tree skirt is the perfect finish to a decorated tree. This shirred tree skirt is simple to make, yet offers an elegant look. It is made from a rectangle of fabric that is shirred up with a decorative cord, creating an attractive ruffled upper edge. The lower edge of the tree skirt is trimmed with fringe or braid trim. The tree skirt can be made to fit a large tree or a tabletop tree.

The large tree skirt has a finished diameter of about 58" (147 cm) and has a 5" (12.5 cm) heading. The tabletop tree skirt measures about 33" (84 cm) across and has a 2½" (6.5 cm) heading. For best results, select a fabric that looks equally good on both sides.

✄ Cutting Directions

For a large tree skirt, cut the length of the fabric to 34" (86.5 cm) wide. Trim the selvage from the remaining long side.

For a tabletop tree skirt, cut a rectangle from fabric, with the length equal to 95" (242 cm) and the width equal to 19" (48.5 cm), piecing as necessary.

YOU WILL NEED

For a large tree skirt:

4⅞ yd. (4.5 m) fabric, for tree skirt.

4⅞ yd. (4.5 m) fringe or braid trim, for embellishment.

4⅞ yd. (4.5 m) decorative cording.

4⅞ yd. (4.5 m) twill tape, ¾" (2 cm) wide.

Liquid fray preventer.

End caps for cording, optional.

For a tabletop tree skirt:

1⅓ yd. (1.27 m) fabric, for tree skirt.

2⅔ yd. (2.48 m) fringe or braid trim, for embellishment.

2⅔ yd. (2.48 m) decorative cording.

2⅔ yd. (2.48 m) twill tape, ¾" (2 cm) wide.

Liquid fray preventer.

End caps for cording, optional.

Tree skirts can be made for full-size or tabletop Christmas trees. The large tree skirt (right) is embellished with braid trim. The tabletop tree skirt (above) features fringe around the outer edge.

How to Sew a Shirred Tree Skirt with a Ruffled Header

1) Turn up ¼" (6 mm) twice on one long side of fabric rectangle. Stitch close to second fold. This side is upper edge of tree skirt.

2) Turn up ¾" (2 cm) twice on short side of fabric rectangle. Stitch close to second fold. Repeat on the other short side. Finish the remaining long edge of fabric rectangle with serger or zigzag stitching.

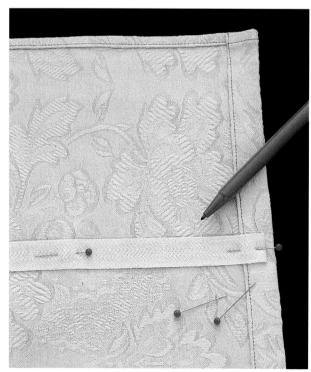

3) Mark line 4¾"(12 cm) from upper edge of tree skirt. Turn under ⅜" (1 cm) on short ends of twill tape. Pin twill tape to tree skirt, ¼" (6 mm) from short edge of tree skirt, aligning one long edge of twill tape with marked line.

4) Stitch close to edge of each side of twill tape, stitching to edges of tree skirt fabric at both ends.

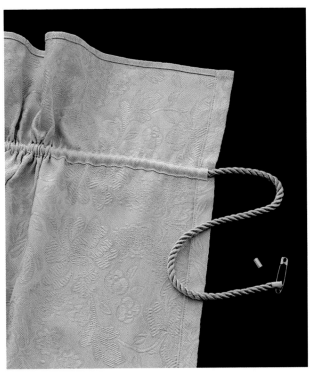

5) Apply liquid fray preventer to cut ends of the trim; allow to dry. Stitch fringe trim to tree skirt ½" (1.3 cm) from lower edge; turn ¾" (2 cm) to back side at ends, and catch in stitching.

6) Insert decorative cording through the twill tape casing. Knot ends, or apply decorative end caps.

7) Tie tree skirt around base of tree above tree stand. Arrange fabric in circle around tree, and arrange ruffle at top so it stands up. Tie cording in bow at back of tree.

Christmas Elves

Display this creative elf on a holiday mantel or buffet table to surprise your guests. The elf is dressed in a sweater made from adult socks. His pants and hat are created from wool coating and are trimmed with white wool. His suspenders, made from leather cording, are finished with gold doll buckles and Ultrasuede®, and his boots are trimmed with small bells at the tips. To embellish the elf further, add a few miniature accessories, such as a small train, boat, or rocking horse, and a paint bucket to keep him busy in Santa's workshop.

✂ Cutting Directions

For the body, cut two 5" × 7" (12.5 × 18 cm) rectangles from muslin. For the arms, cut four 1⅜" × 6¼" (3.5 × 15.7 cm) rectangles from muslin. For the legs, cut two 2¼" × 9" (6 × 23 cm) rectangles from knit fabric and two 2" × 3" (5 × 7.5 cm) rectangles from muslin. Cut the head and ear pieces as on page 40, steps 1 and 2.

For the pants, cut two 5½" × 8" (14 × 20.5 cm) rectangles from wool coating.

For the sweater body, cut 5½" (14 cm) from the top of one adult sock. From the remaining sock, cut two 2½" × 5" (6.5 × 12.5 cm) rectangles, placing the ribbing along one 2½" (6.5 cm) side, for the sleeves. Cut the boots as on page 46, step 27. Cut the suspender trim as on page 45, step 22.

YOU WILL NEED

¼ yd. (0.25 m) muslin.

Scrap of wool coating, for pants and hat.

One pair adult socks, with ½" (1.3 cm) ribbing at top, for sweater.

¼ yd. (0.25 m) knit fabric, for stockings.

2¼ yd. (2.1 m) leather cording, 2 mm wide, for suspenders.

Two doll buckles, for suspenders.

Scrap of Ultrasuede, for boots and suspender trim.

Curly wool doll hair, for hair and beard.

White curly wool doll hair, for trim on pants and hat.

Five chenille stems; wire cutter.

Two 4.5 mm animal eyes.

Cosmetic blush; cotton swab.

6 mm bells, for trim on boots.

Black cotton cording, for ties on boots.

Polyester fiberfill.

Paper-backed fusible web.

⅔ c. (150 mL) sand; plastic bag, such as a sandwich bag.

Thick white craft glue.

Hot glue gun and glue sticks.

Miniature embellishments, such as a toy train, boat, or rocking horse.

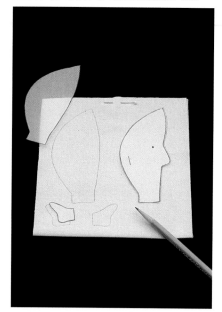

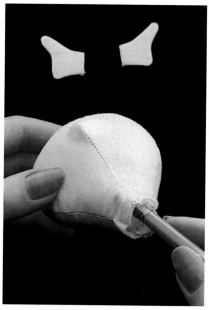

1) Transfer patterns for head and ears (page 47) onto paper; cut on marked lines. Fold piece of muslin in half, right sides together; trace head front, head back, and two ears lightly onto the muslin, using a pencil.

2) Stitch on marked line for center front and center back of the head. Stitch around ear, leaving opening along straight edge. Trim close to stitching, and cut along remaining pencil lines. Turn ear right side out.

3) Pin head front to head back, right sides together; stitch ¼" (6 mm) from raw edges. Trim seam allowances close to stitching. Turn right side out. Stuff head firmly with polyester fiberfill, pushing stuffing into nose. Set head and ears aside.

4) Mark point along one short side of rectangles for body, ⅝" (1.5 cm) from the long sides. Draw lines connecting the points to corners of rectangle on opposite side. Cut on marked lines. Shortest side becomes top of body; longest short side becomes bottom of body.

5) Stitch ¼" (6 mm) from all sides, leaving 2½" (6.5 cm) opening at center of bottom seam. Trim seam allowances close to stitching. Fold fabric, so top body seam aligns with side seams and forms triangles at corners; pin. Mark a line ¾" (2 cm) across corner; repeat for remaining corner at top of body. Stitch on marked lines.

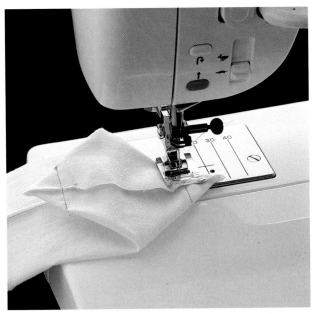

6) Align bottom body seam with side seam to form triangle at lower corner. Mark a line 1½" (3.8 cm) across corner; repeat for remaining lower corner. Stitch on marked lines. Turn right side out. Stuff upper half of body with polyester fiberfill.

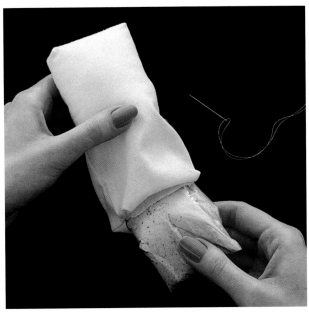

7) Place about ⅔ cup (150 mL) sand in a plastic bag. Tape bag closed, allowing some space inside for sand to shift easily; this makes it easier for elf to sit. Insert bag into body. Stuff remainder of body with polyester fiberfill; hand-stitch opening closed.

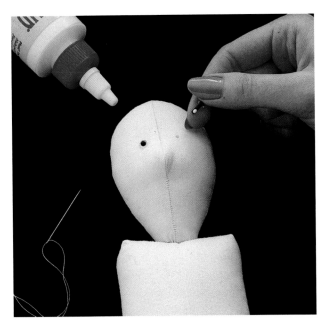

8) Fold ¼" (6 mm) to inside around neck opening. Pin head to center of top of body. Hand-stitch in place. Insert eyes into head at marked points as indicated on pattern; secure with drop of craft glue.

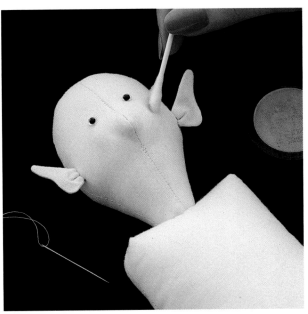

9) Fold ⅛" (3 mm) to inside of ear along straight edge. Hand-stitch opening closed, making a small tuck at center of straight edge. Hand-stitch ear to head at marking as indicated on the pattern. Rub cosmetic blush on cheeks, using a cotton swab.

(Continued on next page)

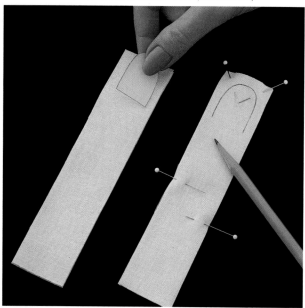

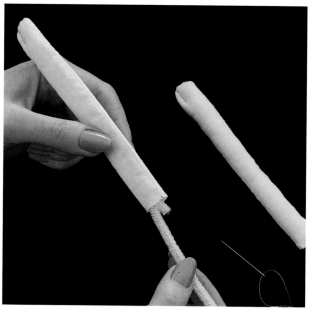

10) Transfer pattern for hand onto paper; cut out. Place two rectangles for arms right sides together; position the pattern for hand ¼" (6 mm) from one short end, and trace lightly, using a pencil. Pin. Stitch ¼" (6 mm) from long edges, following marked line for hand at one short end and leaving remaining short end unstitched. Trim seam allowances close to stitching. Turn arm right side out. Repeat for the remaining arm.

11) Stuff hand lightly with polyester fiberfill. Stitch thumb as indicated on pattern. Fold over ¼" (6 mm) on one end of chenille stem. Insert stem into arm, to end of hand. Stuff remainder of arm with polyester fiberfill. Trim chenille stem even with upper edge of arm; fold over ¼" (6 mm) at end. Turn under ¼" (6 mm) at upper edge of arm; hand-stitch opening closed. Repeat for remaining arm. Hand-stitch arms to body at shoulder side seams.

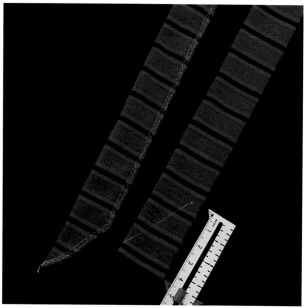

12) Fold rectangle for leg right sides together. Mark point along fold ¼" (6 mm) from one short side. Mark point ¼" (6 mm) from long edge 1¾" (4.5 cm) from same short side. Draw line connecting points. Stitch ¼" (6 mm) from long edge to marked point, using narrow zigzag stitch; pivot, and continue stitching to point. Stitch again close to first stitching. Trim seam allowances close to stitching. Repeat for remaining leg.

13) Turn legs right side out. Fold over ¼" (6 mm) on one end of chenille stem; insert into leg. Stuff leg lightly with polyester fiberfill. Tie matching thread around ankle to cinch in slightly. Knot thread; trim thread tails. Tie matching thread around the center at knee area. Knot thread; trim thread tails. Trim chenille stem even with upper edge of leg; fold over ¼" (6 mm) at end. Repeat for remaining leg.

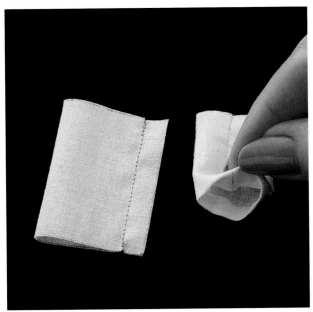

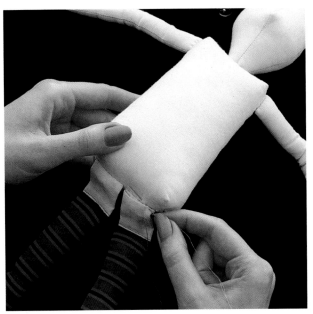

14) Stitch ¼" (6 mm) from upper edge of leg. Fold 2" × 3" (5 × 7.5 cm) rectangle in half to make 1½" × 2" (3.8 × 5 cm) rectangle; stitch ¼" (6 mm) from edge opposite fold. Turn right side out; fold ¼" (6 mm) to inside on each end.

15) Insert leg into one end. Stitch across end close to fold, using a zipper foot. Repeat for remaining leg. Hand-stitch the legs to center bottom of the body, positioning them ¼" (6 mm) from side seams.

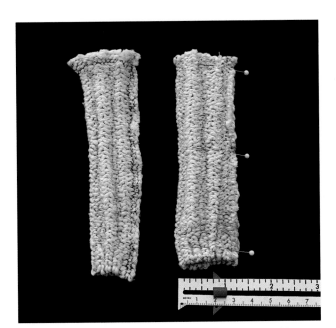

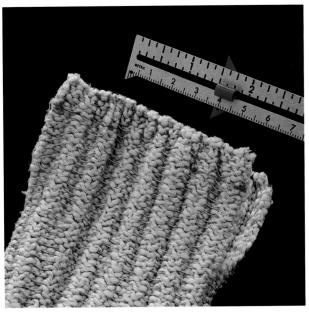

16) Fold rectangle for the sweater sleeve in half lengthwise. Mark point at ribbing edge, ¾" (2 cm) from fold. Mark point ¼" (6 mm) from long edge on opposite short side. Draw line connecting points. Stitch on marked line, using a narrow zigzag stitch. Stitch again just outside previous stitching. Trim close to stitching. Zigzag around armhole opening. Turn right side out. Repeat for remaining sleeve.

17) Turn 5½" (14 cm) sweater tube wrong side out. Cut 2" (5 cm) slit along both folds of the tube at ribbing end. Mark points on each side ½" (1.3 cm) from the ribbed edge. Mark points 1½" (3.8 cm) apart, centered along ribbed edge and ½" (1.3 cm) from ribbed edge, to mark neck opening. Draw lines connecting neck points and lines connecting lower neck point to points at sides as shown.

(Continued on next page)

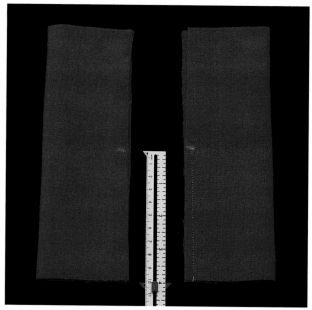

18) Stitch on marked lines, using narrow zigzag stitch. Stitch again close to first stitches; trim. Pin sleeve to armhole opening, right sides together, with sleeve seam at lower edge of armhole. Stitch scant ¼" (6 mm) from raw edges, using narrow zigzag stitch. Zigzag raw edges together. Repeat for the remaining sleeve. Zigzag around the lower edge of the sweater.

19) Fold rectangle for the pants, lengthwise, right sides together. Mark point on edge opposite fold 4" (10 cm) from short side. Stitch from one short side to marked point ¼" (6 mm) from raw edges. Repeat for remaining rectangle.

20) Open upper half of folded rectangles; pin right sides together along remainder of long edges. Stitch from marked point to upper edge on each side. Turn right side out.

21) Topstitch ¼" (6 mm) to the left of center front seam for about 2" (5 cm); stop with needle down. Pivot, angling presser foot diagonally toward center seam; continue stitching to center seam. Fold down ⅜" (1 cm) along upper edge of pants. Stitch ¼" (6 mm) from folded edge.

22) Cut straight line on one side of Ultrasuede® scrap; stitch ⅛" (3 mm) from straight edge. Transfer the pattern for suspender trim to piece of masking tape; cut the pattern from tape. Fold Ultrasuede in half, aligning the stitching line. Position the upper straight edge of tape pattern along the stitching line. Stitch along outer edge of tape through both layers; repeat to stitch three more trim pieces. Trim close to the stitching.

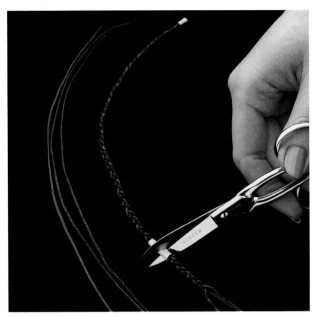

23) Cut leather cording into six equal pieces. Braid three pieces, securing with masking tape at each end. Cut through the masking tape to make a piece 8" (20.5 cm) long; masking tape should cover no more than ¼" (6 mm) of the end. Repeat for the second suspender.

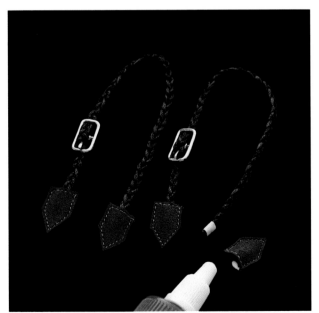

24) Place drop of craft glue inside Ultrasuede trim piece; insert suspender end into trim piece. Position metal doll buckle in place about 1" (2.5 cm) above trim piece. Glue the opposite end of suspender to second trim piece. Repeat for remaining suspender.

25) Transfer pattern for witch hat top (page 81) onto paper; cut one piece, placing dotted line on fold of fabric. Make hat as on page 80, step 14, using ¼" (6 mm) seam allowance. Glue white wool doll hair for trim to lower edge of the hat and lower edges of pants, using hot glue. Roll small ball from wool, and glue to top of hat.

(Continued on next page)

26) Dress elf in sweater and pants. Glue lengths of curly wool to head for hair, beard, and mustache, using hot glue. Glue small pieces of hair above eyes for eyebrows. Glue hat to head.

27) Transfer pattern for elf boot to paper; cut out. Place two pieces of Ultrasuede® right sides together; tape boot pattern to top. Stitch around boot, ending stitching at dot. Cut around boot scant ⅛" (3 mm) from edge of pattern. Turn boot right side out. Repeat for second boot.

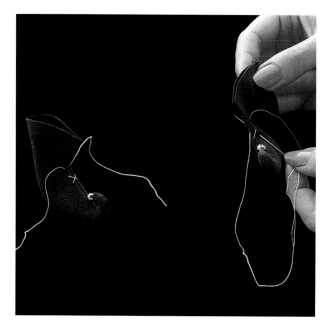

28) Stuff tip of boots with polyester fiberfill. Stitch bell to tip of each boot. Stitch an X across top of boot, stitching ⅛" (3 mm) on each side of seam and ½" (1.3 cm) from opening, using cording; bring ends of lacing out ⅛" (3 mm) on each side of opening.

29) Place boots on feet of elf. Tie cording in bow. Turn down ¾" (2 cm) cuff on top of boots. Hand-stitch suspenders to pants front and back; position the front of suspenders about 1¼" (3.2 cm) from center front seam and the back of suspenders about ¾" (2 cm) from center back seam. Embellish the elf as desired.

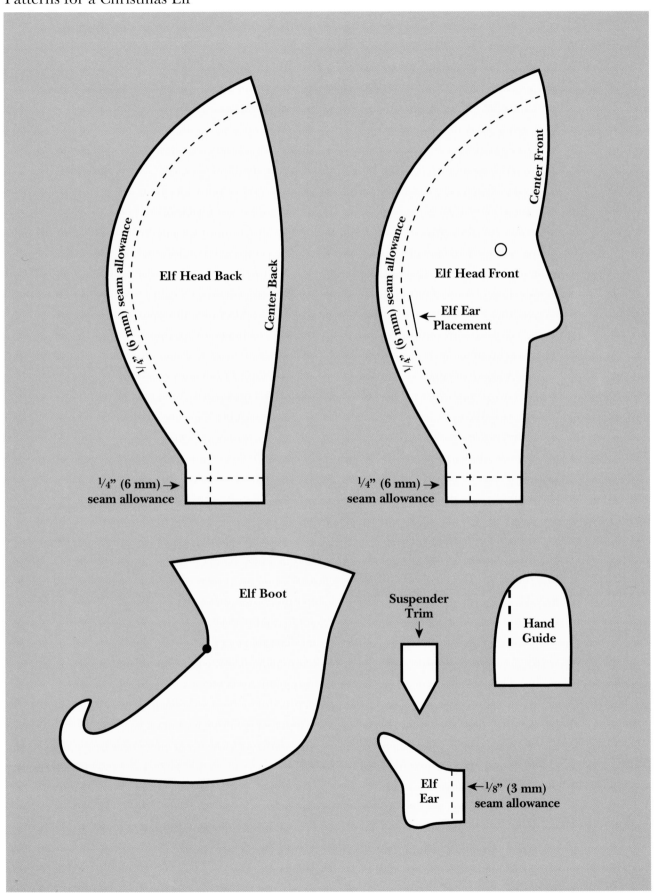

Elf Stockings

Add a touch of whimsy to the holiday festivities by hanging one-of-a-kind elf stockings from your mantel. Make the stocking from decorator fabric and add a contrasting cuff. Or, to use a lighter-weight fabric, simply interface the fabric pieces to give them more body. Decorative cording is laced through eyelets attached to the front of the stocking. Simple eyelet tools and eyelets can be found in most fabric stores. A bell, attached at the end of the toe, adds the finishing touch.

✄ Cutting Directions

Make the full-size pattern (opposite). Cut two stocking pieces from outer fabric and two from lining. For the stocking cuff, cut two 5" × 14¾" (12.5 × 37.4 cm) rectangles from the fabric for the cuff. The rectangles for the cuff are cut to shape on page 50, step 4.

YOU WILL NEED

½ yd. (0.5 m) **outer fabric.**

½ yd. (0.5 m) **lining fabric.**

¼ yd. (0.25 m) **fabric,** for cuff.

½ yd. (0.5 m) **interfacing,** optional.

2 yd. (1.85 m) cording, for lacing and hanger.

End caps for cording, optional.

One ½" (1.3 cm) bell.

Eyelet tool and twelve ⅛" (3 mm) eyelets.

How to Make a Pattern for an Elf Stocking

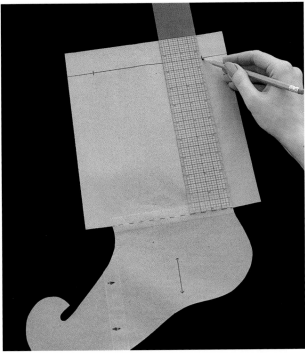

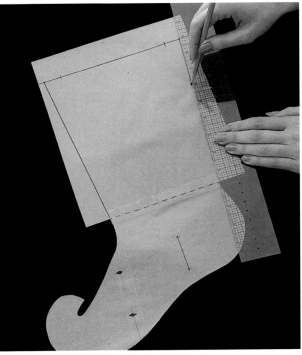

1) Trace partial pattern pieces A and B (page 52) to paper. Tape pieces together, matching notches. Tape a piece of paper to upper edge of partial stocking. Draw a line parallel to and 8½" (21.8 cm) above the dotted line, to mark upper edge of stocking. Align quilter's ruler to dotted line at side; mark point on line for upper edge. Repeat for other side.

2) Measure out ⅞" (2.2 cm) from marked points; mark. Connect outer points at upper edge to sides at ends of dotted line, to make full-size pattern.

How to Sew an Elf Stocking

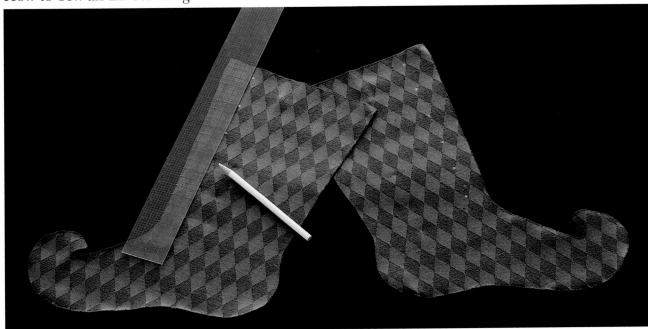

1) Apply interfacing to wrong side of stocking front and back, if desired, following manufacturer's directions. Position edge of ruler 1⅜" (3.5 cm) from the center front at upper edge and 1" (2.5 cm) from center front at location of dotted line on pattern. Mark six points along edge of ruler for eyelets, positioning the first point ⅝" (1.5 cm) from upper edge and each additional point spaced 1⅝" (4 cm) apart. Repeat on other stocking piece.

(Continued on next page)

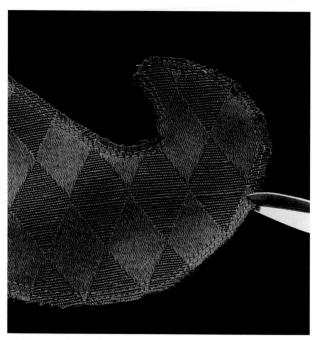

2) Attach eyelets, using eyelet tool and following the manufacturer's directions.

3) Pin stocking front to stocking back, right sides together. Stitch ⅜" (1 cm) seam around stocking, leaving top open; stitch again next to first row of stitching, within seam allowances. Trim the seam allowances close to stitches. Clip curves. Turn the stocking right side out; press lightly.

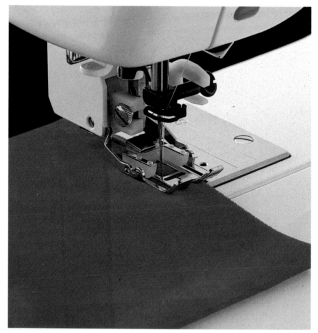

4) Fold the rectangle for cuff in half crosswise, right sides together. Mark a point on the fold 3⅝" (9.3 cm) from upper long edge. Draw line connecting point to corner on lower edge opposite fold. Cut on the marked line. Repeat for remaining rectangle for cuff. Apply interfacing to wrong side of the cuff pieces, if desired, following manufacturer's directions.

5) Pin the cuff pieces right sides together. Stitch ⅜" (1 cm) seam around the sides and lower edge of cuff. Trim seam allowances close to stitching. Turn cuff right side out; press lightly. Baste the upper edges together ¼" (6 mm) from the raw edges.

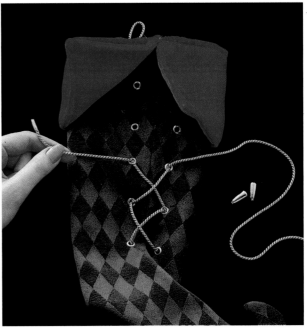

6) Pin upper edge of cuff to stocking, right sides up; overlap the cuff slightly at the center front. Baste cuff to the stocking. Fold 4" (10 cm) length of cording in half for hanger. Baste hanger to the upper edge of right side of stocking.

7) Lace cording through the eyelets; tie bow at top. Attach end caps, if desired. Knot the ends of cording; trim excess.

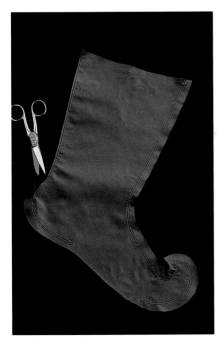

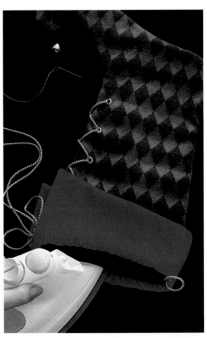

8) Pin the lining pieces right sides together. Stitch ½" (1.3 cm) seam around lining, leaving top open and bottom unstitched 4" to 6" (10 to 15 cm); stitch again next to first row of stitching, within seam allowances. Trim seam allowances close to stitches.

9) Place outer stocking inside the lining, right sides together. Pin and stitch ⅜" (1 cm) from the upper raw edges.

10) Turn stocking right side out through the opening in lining. Slipstitch opening closed; insert lining into stocking. Lightly press upper edge; roll ¼" (6 mm) of cuff to inside of stocking. Hand-stitch bell to the end of the toe.

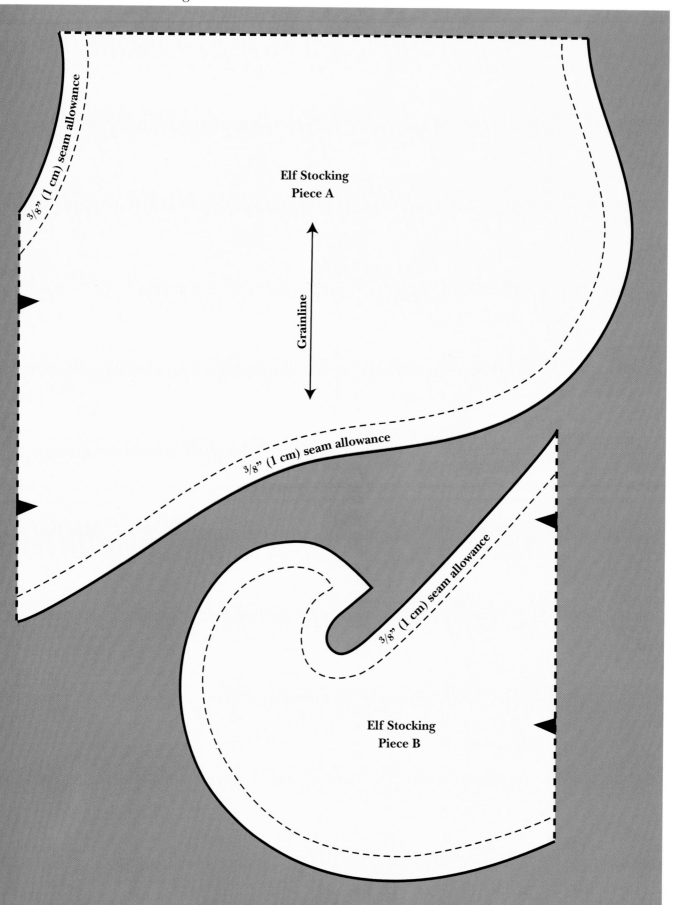

**Elf Stocking
Piece A**

³/₈" (1 cm) seam allowance

Grainline

³/₈" (1 cm) seam allowance

³/₈" (1 cm) seam allowance

**Elf Stocking
Piece B**

Father Christmas Banner

Ring in the spirit of the holidays with a dimensional Father Chrismas wall banner. The banner features padded appliquéd motifs and miniature embellishments, such as children's toys and packages. Hung from a decorative brass rod and cording, the banner is edged with rope welting and finished at the lower point with a tassel. Select fabrics such as taffeta for the sky, cotton velveteen for the snow, and wool coating for the Father Christmas appliqué to give the banner a rich holiday look. The finished banner measures about 18¾" × 34" (47.9 × 86.5 cm) excluding the hanger.

✂ Cutting Directions

Cut one 19½" × 37" (49.8 × 94 cm) rectangle from muslin. Cut one 13½" × 19½" (34.3 × 49.8 cm) rectangle from sky fabric and organza, for the sky. Cut one 4½" × 19½" (11.5 × 49.8 cm) rectangle, one 11½" × 19½" (29.3 × 49.8 cm) rectangle, and one 7" × 19½" (18 × 49.8 cm) rectangle from snow fabric, for the snow. Cut one 11½" × 19½" (29.3 × 49.8 cm) rectangle from the fabric for the lower point of the banner.

Cut one 7" × 13½" (18 × 34.3 cm) rectangle from the Father Christmas garment fabric, backing fabric, and batting, for the Father Christmas.

Cut cottage, roof, trees, snow, and face as on pages 56-57.

Make the patterns as on page 54, step 1, and cut one right and one left boot and two gloves from Ultrasuede®. Cut two pieces from the fabric for the toy bag, using the pattern.

½ yd. (0.5 m) fabric, for sky.

½ yd. (0.5 m) organza, for sky.

½ yd. (0.5 m) fabric, for snow.

⅜ yd. (0.35 m) fabric, for lower point of banner.

⅝ yd. (0.6 m) muslin, for backing of banner front and face of Father Christmas.

Scraps of fabric, for Father Christmas garment, toy bag, cottage, and trees.

Scraps of backing fabrics, for Father Christmas garment, cottage, and trees.

Scrap of felt, for roof of cottage and snow on trees.

⅝ yd. (0.6 m) fabric, for backing of finished banner.

Thin batting, such as Thermore®.

Paper-backed fusible web.

Fur, for trim on Father Christmas garment.

½ yd. (0.5 m) cording, for belt on Father Christmas garment.

Scrap of Ultrasuede®, for boots and gloves.

2¼ yd. (2.1 m) rope welting, for outer edges of banner.

Tassel, for lower point of banner.

1½ yd. (1.4 m) cording, for decorative hanger of banner.

Fine-point permanent-ink marker, for eyes.

Cosmetic blush and cotton swab.

Wool fleece, for hair, beard, and mustache of Father Christmas.

Thick white craft glue.

Miniature embellishments, such as toys.

¼" to ⅜" (6 mm to 1 cm) curtain rod or dowel with finials, about 19" to 20" (48.5 to 51 cm) long without finials.

2 cup hooks, for hanging banner from decorative rod or dowel.

Decorative nail to hang decorative cording on.

How to Sew a Father Christmas Banner

1) **Transfer** Father Christmas garment pieces A and B (pages 60 and 61) to paper; tape them together, matching notches and dotted lines. Transfer the remaining pattern pieces to paper, adding ¼" (6 mm) seam allowance to toy bag. Cut out patterns.

2) **Layer** muslin, sky fabric, and organza rectangles, aligning 19½" (49.8 cm) edges; pin. Baste ⅜" (1 cm) from raw edges on three sides, leaving lower edges of sky fabrics unstitched.

3) Cut wavy line along one long edge of 4½" × 19½" (11.5 × 49.8 cm) rectangle of snow fabric for the background snow piece. Press up ¼" (6 mm) along wavy line. Pin background snow piece to muslin, lapping wavy edge over sky fabrics.

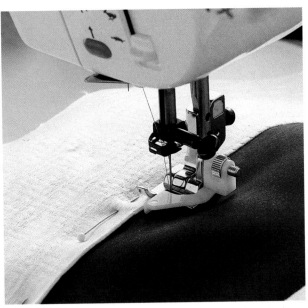

4) Set machine for short blindstitch, with the stitch width about ¹⁄₁₆" (1.5 mm); use monofilament nylon thread in the needle. (Contrasting thread was used to show detail.) Blindstitch along wavy edge of background snow piece, catching edge with widest swing of stitch. Trim excess sky fabric, under snow fabric, ¼" (6 mm) from stitching.

5) Cut curve along upper long edge of 11½" × 19½" (29.3 × 49.8 cm) rectangle of snow fabric to make a hill on the left side of rectangle, for center snow piece. Continue as in steps 3 and 4, lapping center snow piece over background snow piece.

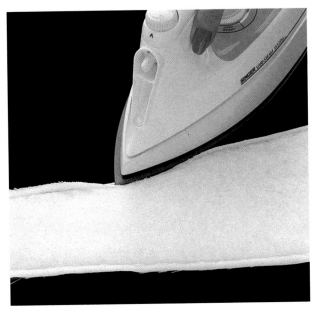

6) Cut curve along upper long edge of 7" × 19½" (18 × 49.8 cm) rectangle of snow fabric to make hill on right side of rectangle for foreground snow piece. Cut the batting, using foreground snow piece as a pattern. Layer foreground snow piece over batting; pin. Baste ¼" (6 mm) from raw edges. Continue as in steps 3 and 4 for foreground snow piece, pressing up ⅜" (1 cm) on upper edge. Baste side edges of snow fabric to muslin, ⅜" (1 cm) from raw edges; baste ½" from lower edge.

(Continued on next page)

7) Pin the backing fabric and cottage fabric right sides together, and place the batting on top. Pin cottage pattern to layered scraps of fabric, reversing the pattern. Stitch around outer edges of the cottage, using a short stitch length. Trim fabric and batting close to the stitching.

8) Cut slit in backing fabric. Turn cottage right side out through slit. Shape cottage along seams, using a point turner. Press. Pin cottage to banner, lapping it over background snow piece by about 1" (2.5 cm). Blindstitch cottage to banner as on page 55, step 4.

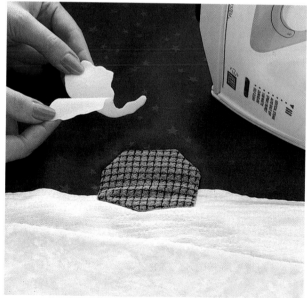

9) Apply paper-backed fusible web to scrap of felt for the cottage roof, following manufacturer's directions. Trace cottage roof to the paper side of fusible web, reversing image. Cut on marked line. Remove paper backing from fusible web. Fuse the roof to cottage, following the manufacturer's directions. Blindstitch around outer edges of roof as on page 55, step 4.

10) Layer backing fabrics, tree fabrics, and batting, with batting on top. Pin tree patterns to rectangles. Stitch around outer edges of pattern. Trim close to stitching. Cut slits in backing fabrics, turn right sides out, shape, and press. Place trees around cottage as shown; blindstitch as on page 55, step 4. Apply snow to trees as for cottage roof in step 9.

11) Layer backing fabric, Father Christmas garment fabric, and batting rectangles, with batting on top. Pin Father Christmas garment pattern to rectangles, reversing the pattern. Stitch around outer edges of pattern. Trim excess fabric and batting close to the stitching. Cut slit in the backing fabric; turn right side out. Shape, and press.

12) Pin Father Christmas garment to front of banner. Pin gloves and boots in place; straight-stitch close to outer edges. Fold cording for the belt in half; insert fold under garment at waist, just under left arm; pin. Blindstitch around Father Christmas garment.

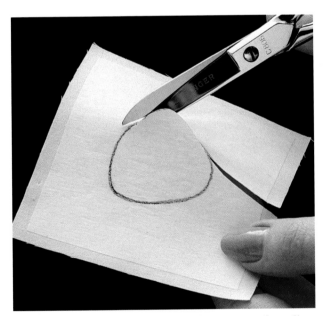

13) Apply paper-backed fusible web to scrap of muslin for face, following manufacturer's directions. Transfer pattern for face to paper side of web, reversing image. Cut on marked line. Remove paper backing, and fuse the face to garment, using the pattern as a guide for placement.

14) Glue wool fleece around face for hair, beard, and mustache. Apply cosmetic blush to cheeks, using a cotton swab. Draw eyes on the Father Christmas as shown. Cut ⅜" (1 cm) fur strip for trim on center front of garment. Secure in place with craft glue.

(Continued on next page)

15) Cut ½" (1.3 cm) fur strips for trim on hat, lower edge of garment, and lower edges of sleeves. Secure in place with craft glue. Position cording across waist; stitch in place on opposite side of waist. Tie at waist, and tie knots at ends; trim excess.

16) Pin toy bag pieces right sides together. Stitch ¼" (6 mm) from raw edges; trim corners and clip curves. Cut slit in lining side of bag near lower edge. Turn right side out through slit. Shape along seamlines with a point turner. Press. Stitch slit on lining side of bag closed. Pin toy bag to banner, allowing ease in bag to make room for toys; position right side of bag in the hand of Father Christmas. Blindstitch toy bag to banner.

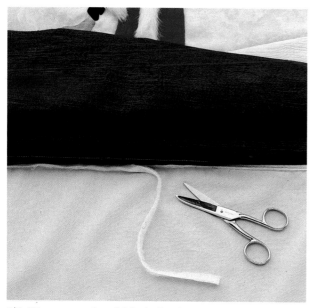

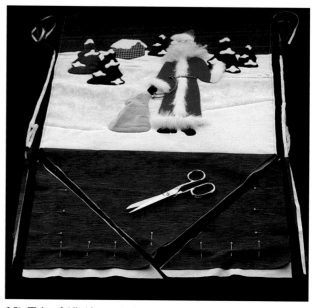

17) Pin rectangle of fabric for lower point to lower edge of snow fabric, right sides together. Stitch ⅝" (1.5 cm) from raw edges, stitching through muslin. Trim excess snow fabric ¼" (6 mm) from stitching; trim the batting close to stitching. Pin lower point fabric to muslin about 1" (2.5 cm) from outer edges.

18) Trim ¼" (6 mm) from each side and top of banner. Mark point at center of lower edge of lower point fabric. Draw lines connecting seamline of lower point fabric and snow fabric to point at lower edge. Cut on the marked lines. Baste around outer edges of lower point fabric, ¼" (6 mm) from raw edges.

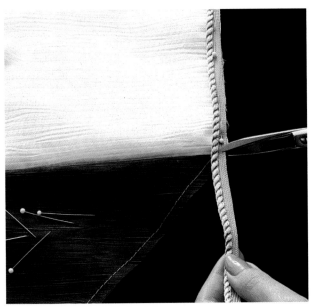

19) Cut the backing fabric to match the banner front. Pin rope welting to outer edges of banner, pinning ends of welting to side edges of banner, ¼" (6 mm) from upper edge of banner, and clipping welting at corners.

20) Baste rope welting to front of banner, using a zipper foot. Pin the backing fabric to banner front, right sides together. Stitch just inside the previous stitching. Stitch along upper edge, ¼" (6 mm) from the raw edges, leaving an opening for turning. Trim the corners.

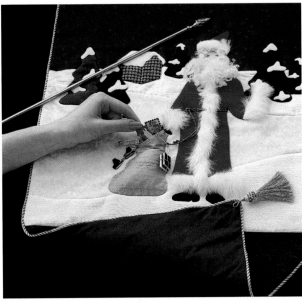

21) Turn banner right side out. Press lightly. Press in ¼" (6 mm) along opening at upper edge. Turn 1" (2.5 cm) to wrong side of banner; pin. Stitch close to the fold. Insert cording through the casing. Stitch the ends of cording for the decorative hanger together; wrap ends tightly with tape. Pull ends into casing to conceal tape.

22) Hand-stitch the tassel to the wrong side of lower point of banner. Embellish banner with miniature toys, securing in place with hand stitches. Insert the curtain rod into the casing. Hang the rod on cup hooks. Secure decorative hanger in place with decorative nail.

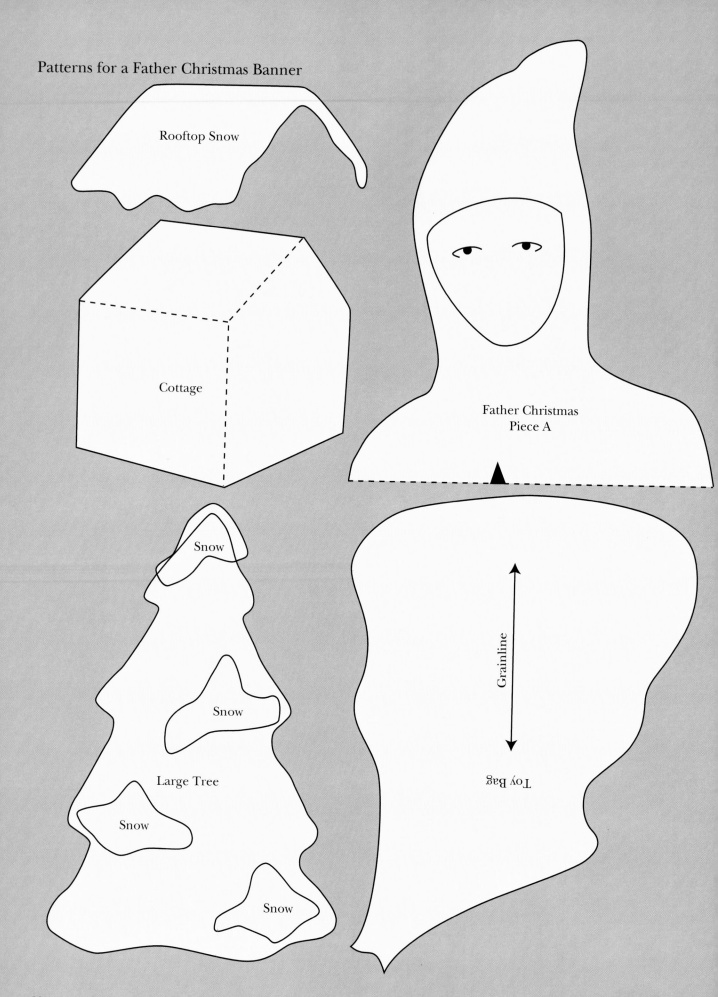

Patterns for a Father Christmas Banner

Rooftop Snow

Cottage

Father Christmas
Piece A

Snow

Snow

Large Tree

Snow

Snow

Grainline

Toy Bag

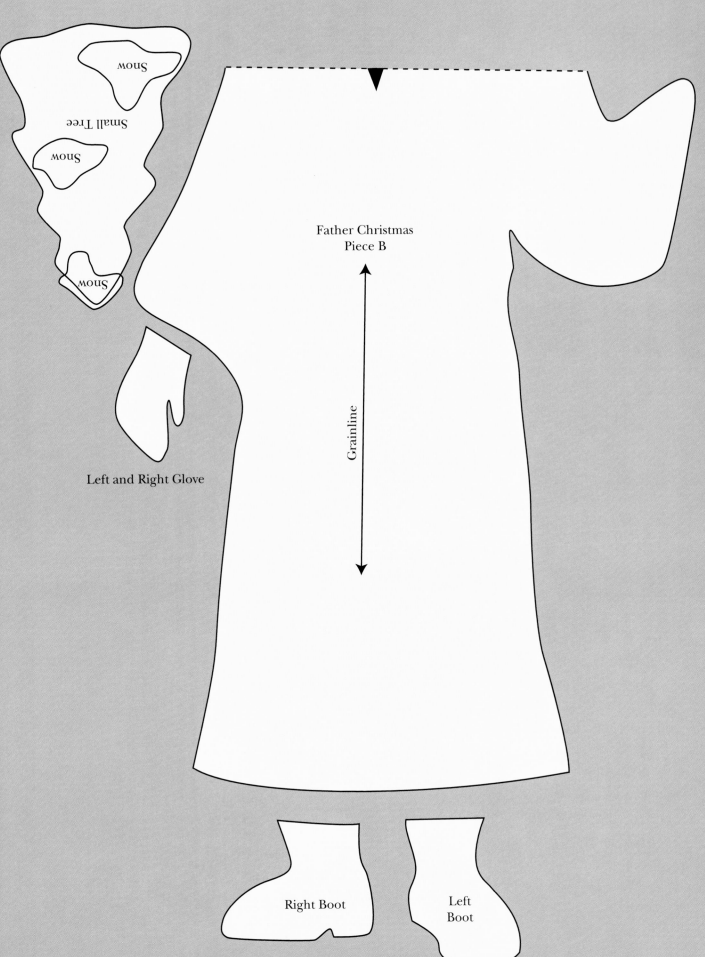

Snow

Snow

Small Tree

Snow

Father Christmas
Piece B

Grainline

Left and Right Glove

Right Boot

Left
Boot

Cards & Gift Tags

Make your own customized cards and gift tags for the special people on your holiday list. Cards are easily created from card stock or heavyweight stationery, available at office supply stores. Heavyweight papers may need to be scored before folding. Or, you can use blank greeting cards and matching envelopes, available at many craft stores.

Choose from a variety of card styles, shown from top to bottom, left to right: card with hand-stitched fabric motif, card with a fabric collage, card with fabric cutouts, gift tag with hand-stitched felt motif, and card with quilted window opening. Combine any of the techniques to design your own card. Use holiday cookie cutters as patterns for motifs, or draw your own freehand holiday designs. Embellish cards or tags with charms, buttons, ribbons, or miniature decorations.

YOU WILL NEED

Card stock or heavyweight stationery.

Scraps of fabric.

Scraps of fabric with printed holiday motifs, for card with fabric cutouts.

Buttons, charms, beads, or ribbon, for embellishing, optional.

Mat knife and cutting surface, for card with window opening and card with bow.

Scrap of batting, for card with window opening and card with hand-stitched fabric motif.

Embroidery floss, for card with hand-stitched fabric or felt motif.

Permanent-ink marking pens.

Thick white craft glue.

How to Make a Card or Gift Tag from Fabric Cutouts

1) Apply paper-backed fusible web to scrap of motif fabric and background fabric, following manufacturer's directions. Cut the desired motif from paper-backed fabric. Peel off the paper, and fuse motif to the background fabric. Trim background fabric around motif as desired. Peel off the paper from background fabric, and fuse to front of card or gift tag.

2) Write greeting on the card, using permanent-ink marking pen. Embellish card, if desired, with bow by cutting two slits in card, ¼" (6 mm) apart, using a mat knife. Insert ribbon through slits, and tie bow. Stitch charm to bow, if desired.

How to Make a Card or Gift Tag with a Hand-stitched Motif

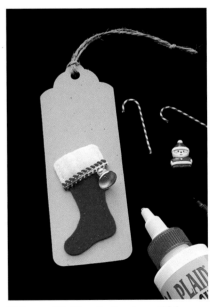

Fabric motif. 1) Follow step 1, above, cutting a square or rectangle from fabric in place of a motif. Apply paper-backed fusible web to scrap of fabric for padded motif. Draw desired motif on paper side of fusible web, reversing image; cut out motif. Peel off paper, and fuse motif to scrap of batting. Trim excess batting around edges of motif.

2) Hand-stitch motif to card, ⅛" (3 mm) from outer edges of motif, using hand running stitches and two or three strands of embroidery floss. Hand-stitch buttons to card for embellishment, if desired. Glue scrap of paper to the inside front cover to conceal the stitching.

Felt motif. Cut desired motif from felt. Hand-stitch motif to card, ⅛" (3 mm) from outer edges of motif, using hand running stitches and two or three strands of embroidery floss. Secure any embellishments to card. Write greeting on card, using a permanent-ink marking pen.

How to Make a Quilted Card with a Window Opening

1) Piece the fabrics as on page 19, steps 1 and 2, omitting the reference to interfacing in step 1 and reference to steps 1 to 7 in step 2. Layer the pieced fabric over scrap of batting; stitch along seamlines through both layers, stitching in the well of the seam.

2) Trace desired design for window to inside front cover of card. Cut on the marked lines, using a mat knife. Cut pieced fabric and batting scant ¼" (6 mm) smaller than dimensions of card front. Tape pieced fabric to inside front of card over opening.

3) Machine zigzag-stitch ¼" (6 mm) from the outer edges of the card front. Lift needle, and reposition at corners as necessary to stay ¼" (6 mm) from edge of card. Pull threads to inside, and knot.

4) Apply glue to inside front of the card; press card closed to conceal batting and tape. Cut the front from second card, ¾" (2 cm) from fold of card. Apply glue to ¾" (2 cm) strip, and glue to back of card front with window opening, aligning folds; weight with heavy object until glue is dry.

How to Make a Card or Gift Tag with a Fabric Collage

1) Fuse fabric scraps to front of fabric for foreground collage as desired, using fusible web and following manufacturer's directions. Stitch randomly as desired on foreground collage fabric, using decorative thread. Cut rectangle from collage ¼" (6 mm) larger on all sides than desired finished size.

2) Apply fusible web to piece of card stock, cut to the desired size of foreground collage. Center and fuse the foreground collage fabric to rectangle of card stock. Turn the edges of foreground fabric to the back of card stock; press. Trim excess fabric at the corners, if desired.

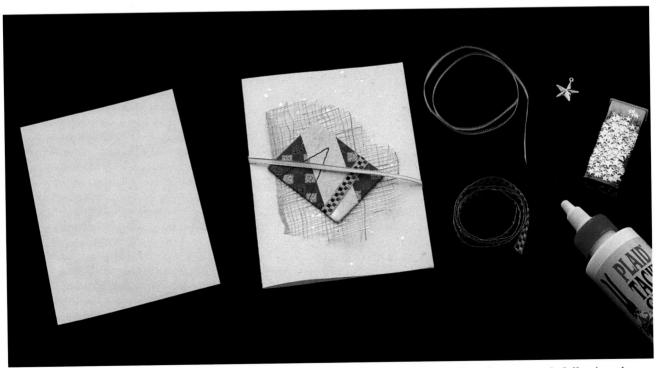

3) Cut scrap from background fabric; stitch to card if using nonfusable material, or fuse to card, following the manufacturer's directions. Glue foreground collage to front of card as desired. Glue ribbons or other trim to card as desired. Weight card until glue is dry. Stitch beads or charms to the card as desired. Glue scrap of paper to inside front cover to conceal stitching.

Halloween

Quilted Halloween Wall Hanging

Decorate your home for Halloween with this wall hanging, depicting four traditional Halloween scenes. The wall hanging is divided into four blocks; the cat block, ghost block, pumpkin block, and bat block. The blocks are framed with sashing strips and a border. Tabs at the top are used to hang the quilt from a crooked twig.

The Halloween scenes are created by fusing design motifs to a background block. When fusing light-colored fabrics to dark backgrounds, the background may show through. To prevent show-through, fuse two layers of light-colored fabric together, using fusible web, to create a more opaque finish.

To add some dimensional characteristics to the quilt, green floral wire is used to make the curly vine on the pumpkin. The spider web is an overlay, created by satin stitching over cotton cording. And sitting on the spider web is a rubber spider. Use your imagination to add dimensional features to the quilt.

✂ Cutting Directions

Cut four 8½" (21.8 cm) squares from the desired fabrics for the skies.

Cut one 1½" × 8½" (3.8 × 21.8 cm) rectangle from the fabric for the foreground of the cat block. Cut one 4" × 8½" (10 × 21.8 cm) rectangle from the fabric for the foreground of the pumpkin block. Cut one 5" × 8½" (12.5 × 21.8 cm) rectangle from the

fabric for the foreground of the ghost block. Cut one 4½" × 8½" (11.5 × 21.8 cm) rectangle from the brick fabric for the foreground of the bat block.

Cut two 2½" × 8½" (6.5 × 21.8 cm) strips and one 2½" × 18½" (6.5 × 47.3 cm) strip from sashing fabric. Cut two 2½" × 18½" (6.5 × 47.3 cm) strips and two 2½" × 22½" (6.5 × 57.3 cm) strips for the border. Cut five 4½" (11.5 cm) squares from the fabric for the tabs. Cut one 26" (66 cm) square from muslin. Cut the backing as on page 73, step 20.

YOU WILL NEED

¼ yd. (0.25 m) each of two or three sky fabrics.

Scraps of fabric, for cat, half moon, fence, ghost, tombstones, tree, pumpkins, brick wall, bat, full moon and foregrounds.

1 yd. (0.95 m) fabric, for sashing, border, tabs, and backing.

¾ yd. (0.7 m) muslin.

Batting, about 26" (66 cm) square.

Green paddle floral wire, for vines on pumpkins.

#5 cotton cording, for spider web.

Water-soluble stabilizer, for spider web.

Plastic or rubber spider, about ½" (1.3 cm) long.

Paper-backed fusible web.

Fine-point permanent-ink marking pen.

Crooked twig, such as curly willow or birch, for hanger.

How to Sew a Quilted Halloween Wall Hanging

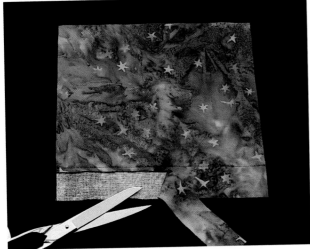

1) Pin foreground rectangle for cat block to square of sky fabric, matching lower edges. Stitch close to upper edge of foreground piece. Trim away excess sky fabric behind foreground a scant ¼" (6 mm) from stitching.

2) Cut wavy line along one long edge of foreground piece for the pumpkin block. Continue as in step 1. Cut wavy line along one long edge of the foreground rectangle for the ghost block to create a steep curve on one half of the strip. Continue as in step 1. Trim away a few bricks at the upper edge of foreground rectangle for the bat block. Continue as in step 1.

(Continued on next page)

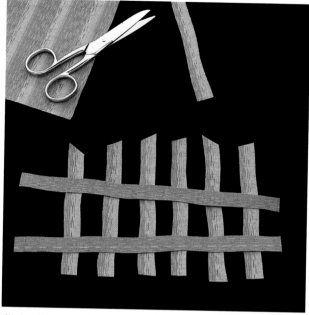

3) Apply paper-backed fusible web to scraps of fabric for design motifs, following manufacturer's directions. Trace the patterns (pages 74 and 75) onto paper. Cut 3½" (9 cm) circle for the moon. Transfer the designs onto paper side of fusible web. Cut design motifs from paper-backed fusible web. Apply any details to motifs, using fine-point permanent-ink marking pen.

4) Apply paper-backed fusible web to scrap of fabric for fence. Cut wavy strips from paper-backed fence fabric about ½" (1.3 cm) wide. Cut two fence rails 8½" (21.8 cm) long and cut seven fence posts about 4½" (11.5 cm) long; vary the lengths slightly, and cut one short end diagonally.

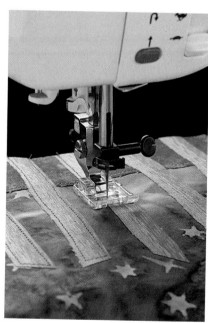

5) Fuse fence posts to cat block, aligning lower edges of posts with lower edge of block. Position some of the posts to appear slightly tilted. Stitch close to raw edges of posts.

6) Fuse fence rails over fence posts, positioning one rail over stitching line of foreground rectangle and one about ½" (1.3 cm) from upper edges of posts. Fuse half-moon to the right-hand corner of block, and fuse cat to block so feet rest on top fence rail.

7) Fuse the ghost and tombstones to ghost block as shown. Fuse the tree and pumpkins to pumpkin block, and fuse moon and bat to bat block as shown.

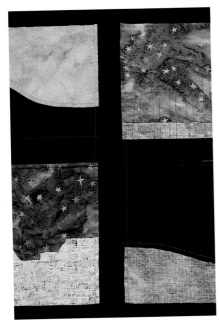

8) Stitch 8½" (21.8 cm) sashing strip between cat and pumpkin blocks, using ¼" (6 mm) seam allowances; press seam allowances toward sashing strip. Repeat for ghost and bat blocks. Stitch 18½" (47.3 cm) sashing strip between pairs of blocks; press seam allowances toward sashing strip.

9) Stitch short outer borders to upper and lower edges of quilt; press the seam allowances toward borders. Stitch long border strips to sides of quilt; press the seam allowances toward borders. Layer muslin, batting, and quilt top. Pin-baste about every 6" (15 cm).

10) Stitch in the ditch of the seams of the sashing and borders, using a walking foot. Baste layers together a scant ¼" (6 mm) from edges of quilt top.

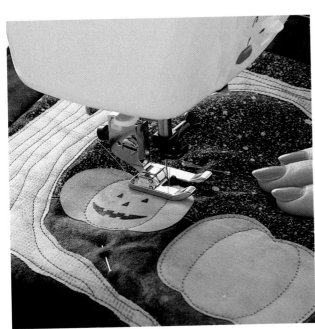

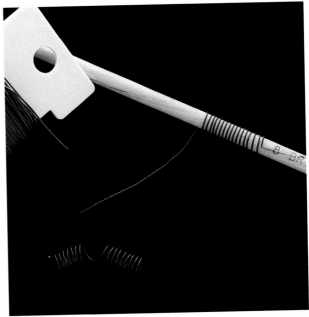

11) Stitch close to edges of all fused appliqués. Stitch additional design lines across sky of ghost block and bricks of bat block to quilt the layers together. Stitch design lines on tree and pumpkins.

12) Cut two 8" to 12" (20.5 to 30.5 cm) lengths of green floral wire, using wire cutter. Twist wire around small-diameter rod, such as a knitting needle, to make wire spiral. Straighten spirals at centers for about ½" (1.3 cm).

(Continued on next page)

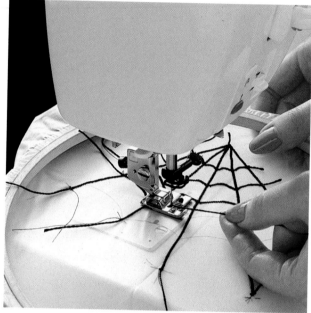

13) Satin stitch stems on the pumpkins, using wide, closely spaced zigzag stitches that narrow slightly at the tops of stems; begin and end stitching with stitch length set at zero, and catch centers of wire spirals in stitching at base of stems. Shape spirals.

14) Transfer spider web pattern (page 74) onto water-soluble stabilizer, using pen. Determine end points of straight lines of spider web, and mark on stabilizer. Insert stabilizer into embroidery hoop; place under needle of sewing machine, with stabilizer against throat plate. Stitch narrow, closely spaced zigzag stitches over cotton cord, using cording foot and following design lines of spider web; stitch straight lines first, then curved lines.

15) Apply drop of liquid fray preventer to ends of stitching lines. Trim stabilizer close to stitching, and remove remaining stabilizer by fusing spider web between wet sheets of paper toweling, following the manufacturer's directions. Allow spider web to dry.

16) Stitch tree to ghost block by using about five rows of narrow satin stitching for trunk and straight stitching for branches.

17) Pin spider web to lower right corner of the bat block. Tack spider web in place at corner of block. Stitch over end points of straight lines of the spider web, using satin stitches, starting ¼" (6 mm) from ends; begin and end stitching with stitch length set at zero. Hand-stitch spider to spider web around center of body.

18) Fold one tab in half, right sides together; stitch ¼" (6 mm) seam along edge opposite fold. Press seam allowances open. Turn the tab right side out, centering seam on back of tab; press. Repeat for remaining tabs. Trim batting and muslin even with edges of pieced quilt top.

19) Fold tabs in half, with seams to inside, matching the raw edges. Pin the tabs to upper edge on right side of quilt front, placing one tab ¼" (6 mm) from each side and spacing remaining tabs evenly across top; baste.

20) Measure finished size of wall hanging; cut the backing piece to this measurement. Pin wall hanging front to backing fabric, right sides together. Stitch ¼" (6 mm) from raw edges, leaving 12" (30.5 cm) opening for turning; trim corners. Turn wall hanging right side out; press. Slipstitch opening closed.

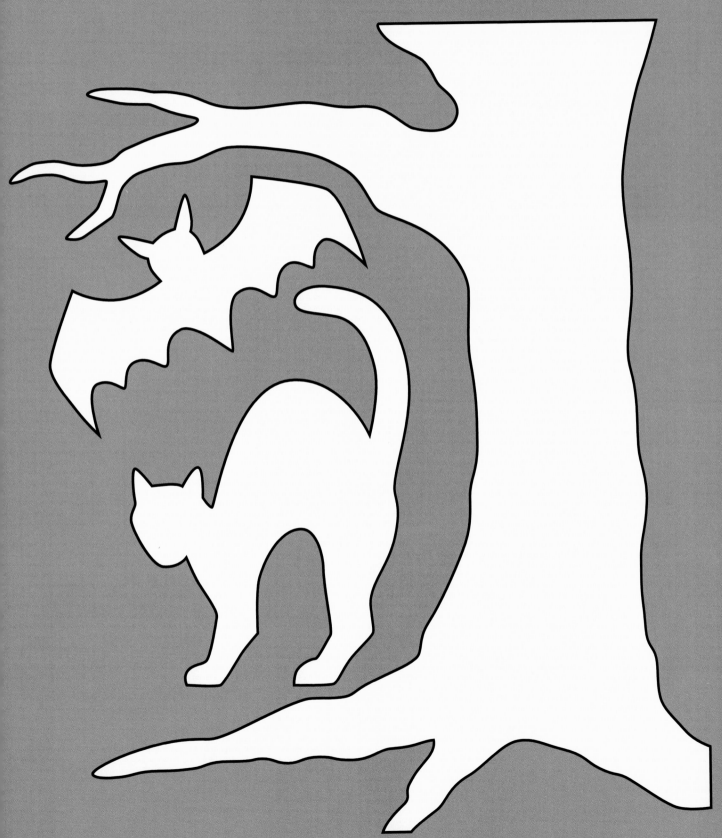

Witch on a Stick

Make this Halloween witch on a stick to greet the trick-or-treaters at your door. She can be posed in a bucket of Halloween candy, or let her stand up by placing her stick in a recycled bottle filled with unpopped popcorn. This friendly witch has long, wired fingers so she can hold her broom close by. The witch's broom is made from a crooked twig. Curly willow is naturally crooked and makes a good choice. The end of the broom is created from lengths of jute that are frayed at one end.

Curly gray wool is used for the witch's hair, and a clear bead stitched to her nose becomes a wart. The witch's dress is made from rectangles of fabric that are cut at ½" (1.3 cm) intervals to create the fringed effect. For contrast, use more than one fabric for the fringed dress, possibly selecting one shiny fabric and one dull fabric or one black fabric and one colored fabric.

✂ Cutting Directions

Cut one 7" (18 cm) square from the fabric for the head front. The head front is cut opposite, in steps 1 and 2. The head back is cut opposite, in step 1. Cut four hand pieces as on page 78, step 5.

Cut three 11" × 26" (28 × 66 cm) rectangles from the fabric for the dress. Also cut one 6½" × 14½" (16.3 × 36.8 cm) rectangle for the sleeves.

Transfer the hat patterns (opposite, step 1), and cut one hat top piece and one hat brim piece from felt. Cut slashes in the brim piece as indicated on the pattern.

¼ yd. (0.25 m) fabric, for head and hands.

⅞ yd. (0.8 m) fabric, for dress.

2 yd. (1.85 m) ribbon, ¼" (6 mm) wide, for drawstring of dress.

¼ yd. (0.25 m) ribbon, ⅜" (1 cm) wide, for embellishing hat.

Curly wool gray doll hair.

Beads, for eyes and wart.

Dowel, ¼" (6 mm) in diameter, cut to 13" (33 cm) long.

Black craft paint; paintbrush.

Felt, for hat.

11 chenille stems, 12" (30.5 cm) long; wire cutter.

Polyester fiberfill.

Red fine-point permanent-ink marker, for mouth.

Cosmetic blush; cotton swab.

Decorative button or metal jewelry finding, for embellishing hat.

Crooked twig, such as curly willow, about 13" (33 cm) long, for broom handle.

Jute, for broom.

Hot glue gun and glue sticks.

How to Make a Halloween Witch on a Stick

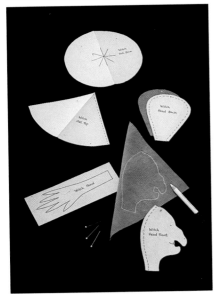  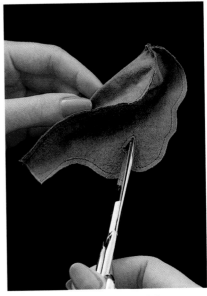

1) **Transfer** patterns for head, hat, and hand pieces (page 81) onto paper, placing any dotted foldlines on the fold of the paper; transfer markings and dot. Cut one head back piece. Fold 7" (18 cm) square of fabric for head in half diagonally, right sides together; pin head front pattern to fabric. Trace around outer edges of pattern; remove pattern.

2) **Stitch** on marked line for center front of face. Trim excess fabric ⅛" (3 mm) from the stitching. Cut on remaining pencil lines.

3) **Pin** head back to head front, right sides together, matching the dot on back piece to seam of front pieces. Stitch ¼" (6 mm) from raw edges. Trim the seam allowances to ⅛" (3 mm). Clip seam allowances on head pieces around curves. Turn head right side out.

(Continued on next page)

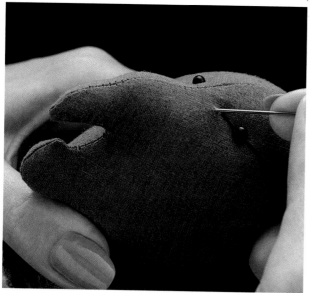

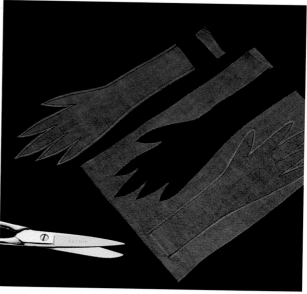

4) Stuff head with polyester fiberfill, using eraser end of a pencil; stuff tightly, including the neck. Stitch bead at marking for eye; insert needle to the opposite side of face, and stitch remaining bead in place, pulling thread tight between the beads to create indentation.

5) Place the fabric for hands wrong sides together. Pin pattern for hands to fabric; trace around outer edges of the pattern. Repeat for second hand. Stitch on marked lines, leaving wrist open. Cut around the hands, about 1/16" (1.5 mm) from stitching.

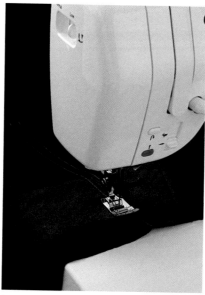

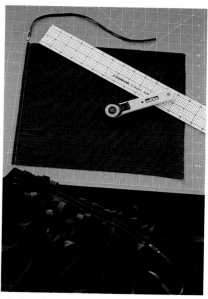

6) Fold 1/4" (6 mm) over on the end of chenille stems, and insert one into each finger. Push the arm fabric down, and twist the chenille stems at the wrist. Repeat for the other hand. Overlap the chenille stem arms about 6" (15 cm), and twist together at center. Set aside until step 11.

7) Layer two rectangles of fabric for dress. Stitch across 11" (28 cm) width of fabric, a scant 1/4" (6 mm) from each side of center, to make casing. Fold remaining rectangle for the dress in half crosswise; stitch 1/4" (6 mm) from the fold to make the casing.

8) Cut 1/2" (1.3 cm) fringe on short edges of layered fabric rectangles, from the raw edges to within 1/4" (6 mm) of each side of the casing. Repeat to make fringe on remaining rectangle. Insert length of ribbon through each casing.

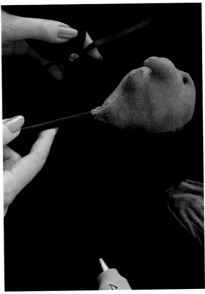

9) Fold rectangle for the sleeves, lengthwise; stitch ¼" (6 mm) from long raw edges. Turn right side out. Paint dowel; allow to dry.

10) Apply hot glue to end of dowel; insert into neck. Using eraser end of a pencil, press neck fabric next to dowel; allow glue to dry.

11) Insert arms into fabric tube for sleeves. Tie 10" (25.5 cm) length of ribbon around sleeve tube and arms at center back; knot ribbon. Apply dot of glue to center of sleeves over knot; secure sleeve and arms to the dowel at back neck area of witch; allow to dry. Tie ribbon from sleeves around front of dowel; tie knot.

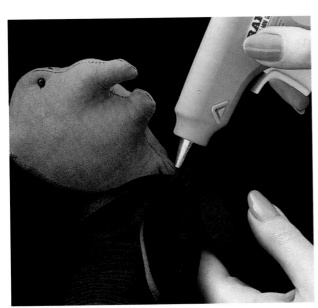

12) Draw up the ribbon on fringed fabric rectangles. Apply glue to the dowel just under sleeves. Tie the single-layer fringed fabric rectangle around dowel, under sleeves, securing with hot glue. Tie the ribbon in knot. Secure with hot glue; allow to dry. Trim off ends of ribbon.

13) Tie the double-layer fringed fabric rectangle around neck of witch, at back; secure with hot glue. Tie the ribbon in knot; trim off ends. Secure lengths of doll hair to head, using hot glue. Secure hat brim to the head, using hot glue.

(Continued on next page)

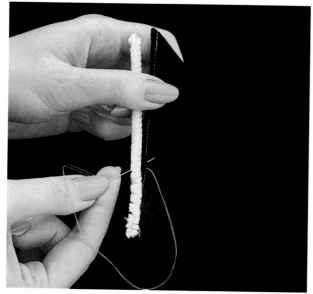

14) Fold the hat top piece in half; stitch ⅛" (3 mm) from straight edge. Cut chenille stem to length of straight side plus ¼" (6 mm). Bend ¼" (6 mm) of each end of chenille stem down. Whipstitch chenille stem to seam allowance. Turn hat piece right side out.

15) Apply hot glue to inside lower edge of hat top piece; glue hat top to the head over center of brim piece. Stitch bead to end of nose for wart. Draw the mouth on witch as indicated on pattern, using fine-point permanent-ink marker. Apply cosmetic blush to cheeks of witch, using a cotton swab.

16) Cut several 5" (12.5 cm) lengths of jute. Hold the bundle of jute around the end of crooked twig. Wrap additional length of jute around bundle, beginning about ¾" (2 cm) from upper edge of bundle. Secure the end of binding thread by threading it through a needle and taking a stitch through binding; trim end.

17) Secure jute to twig with drop of hot glue. Unravel ends of jute for a frayed look.

18) Glue ⅜" (1 cm) ribbon to the hat, just above brim; trim excess. Secure button or metal jewelry finding to ribbon on hat, using hot glue. Bend chenille stem at top of arm to form shoulder. Shape arms and hands to hold broom. Bend top of hat over.

Patterns for Witch on a Stick

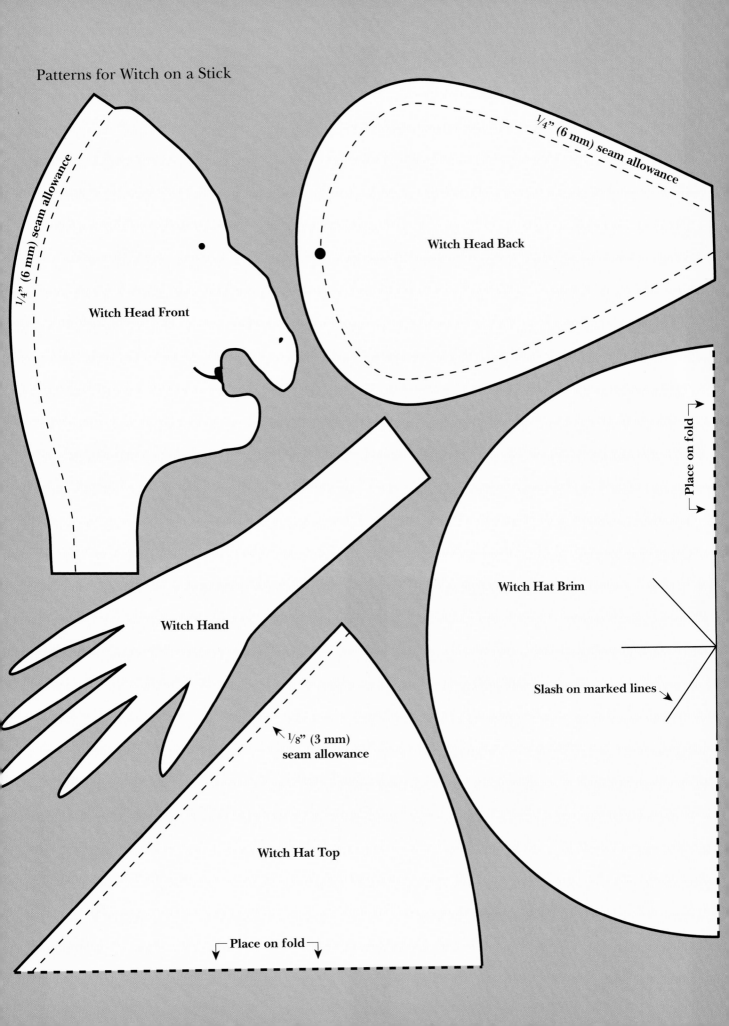

¼" (6 mm) seam allowance

¼" (6 mm) seam allowance

Witch Head Front

Witch Head Back

Place on fold

Witch Hat Brim

Slash on marked lines

Witch Hand

⅛" (3 mm) seam allowance

Witch Hat Top

Place on fold

More Projects for Halloween

Basket liner (page 103) decorates a basket filled with Halloween treats.

Card (page 62), made using the Halloween cat pattern on page 75, invites guests to a Halloween party. Heat-activated pop-up lettering is used for the greeting.

Halloween garlands are variations of the Christmas garlands on page 30. Halloween motifs are combined with buttons, beads, and fabric yo-yos.

Halloween tree made from lichen-covered branches is decorated with felt pumpkins, created by stitching two layers of felt together, using hand running stitches. Cat and bat ornaments are made as on page 32. Hangers are made from lengths of black raffia. Patterns for motifs are from pages 74 and 75. To add to the Halloween mood, synthetic spider webs are draped through the tree.

Thanksgiving

Autumn Harvest Wall Arrangement

Make an everlasting autumn wall arrangement, using authentic-looking fabric gourds and multicolored corn. The fabric gourds and corn are stitched to a raffia braid, concealed behind a bundle of raffia. To vary the design of the gourds, the neck of the gourds can be lengthened or shortened. The position of the seam joining the green and gold fabric can also be varied. A wire chenille stem in the gourd allows the neck to be bent to the desired shape.

The corn is made from multicolored fabric, quilted in both directions, using wavy stitching lines. The corn husks are created from two layers of tea-dyed muslin, stitched at ⅛" to ¼" (3 to 6 mm) intervals. Auburn-colored doll hair is used to make the corn silk at the end of each ear of corn. A cluster of ribbon loops embellishes the top of the arrangement. Hang the arrangement from the twisted loops of raffia at the top.

✂ Cutting Directions

Cut one 6½" × 8½" (16.3 × 21.8 cm) rectangle from a scrap of corn fabric, and from muslin and batting, for each ear of corn. Cut two 7" × 9" (18 × 23 cm) rectangles from muslin for corn husks, for each ear of corn.

Cut one 6" × 11" (15 × 28 cm) rectangle from gold or yellow-orange fabric and one 3½" × 11" (9 × 28 cm) rectangle from green fabric, for each gourd.

YOU WILL NEED

Scraps of three to five fabrics, for corn.

Scraps of green fabric, for gourds.

Scraps of gold or yellow-orange fabric, for gourds.

Batting.

Polyester fiberfill.

Auburn wavy doll hair, for corn silk.

Muslin, for corn husks and for backing of corn.

One chenille stem, for each gourd.

One-half of a 16-oz. (450 g) bundle of raffia.

5 yd. (4.6 m) ribbon.

Upholstery needle and carpet thread or buttonhole twist.

How to Tea-dye Fabric

Brew strong tea, about four tea bags per 1 qt. (1 L) of water; remove tea bags. Soak fabric in tea until desired color is achieved; fabric will be lighter after it has dried. Remove fabric from tea, and squeeze out excess; do not rinse. Place fabric on paper towel; allow to dry. Press fabric to heat-set color; use scrap of fabric to protect ironing surface from any excess tea.

How to Sew an Ear of Corn from Fabric

1) Layer rectangles of muslin for corn husks. Stitch lengthwise through center of rectangles. Stitch again, 1/8" to 1/4" (3 to 6 mm) away on each side of stitching. Repeat to stitch lines over entire rectangle; stitch every other row in the opposite direction. Tea-dye stitched corn husk rectangle, if desired (left).

2) Cut rectangle lengthwise into 2" (5 cm) strips. Trim one end of the strips to a sharp point. Trim the sides of opposite ends, leaving 7/8" (2.2 cm) width along lower edges as shown. Stretch and twist husks to curl husks and fray edges slightly. Set aside husks until step 8.

3) Layer rectangle of corn fabric, batting, and muslin, with the corn fabric on top. Stitch lengthwise through the center of layers, making wavy stitching line. Stitch 1/4" (6 mm) to the right of first stitching. Repeat to quilt the entire rectangle with wavy stitching lines; stitch every other row in the opposite direction.

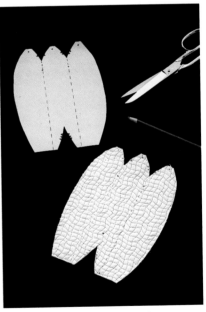

4) Stitch wavy lines crosswise over the layered rectangles as in step 3. Trace pattern for corn (page 91) onto paper. Cut corn from quilted rectangle, using pattern. Transfer markings to the batting side of quilted fabric.

(Continued on next page)

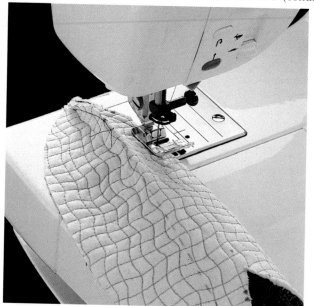

5) Fold fabric for corn right sides together along dotted line as indicated on pattern, matching single notches. Stitch seam at the top of corn from dot to fold, using ¼" (6 mm) seam allowance; stitch three additional stitches at end of seam, stitching straight along fold. Repeat for seam with double notches.

6) Fold fabric for corn in half at bottom, right sides together, matching triple notches. Stitch seam as in step 5. Insert length of wavy doll hair at upper point of corn; stitch to seam allowance.

7) Pin corn along remaining seam; stitch from dot to the lower edge of corn, using ¼" (6 mm) seam allowance. Trim seam allowances close to stitching. Turn corn right side out. Stuff with polyester fiberfill to within ¾" (2 cm) of bottom, using the eraser end of a pencil.

8) Press the lower edges of corn together, centering the seam on back side; stitch ¼" (6 mm) from lower raw edges, using zipper foot. Overlap two corn husk sections at center front at lower edge of corn; wrap excess to the back side of corn at the sides, and pin. Stitch ¼" (6 mm) from the lower edges; trim to ⅛" (3 mm).

How to Sew a Gourd from Fabric

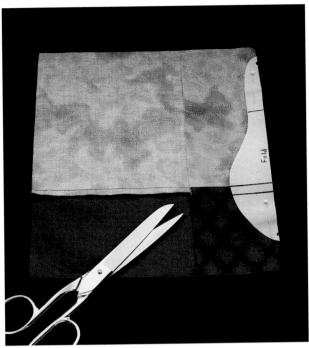

1) Trace gourd pattern (page 91) onto paper. Stitch rectangle of gold or yellow-orange fabric to rectangle of green fabric along one long edge. Press the seam allowances toward the green fabric. Position pattern on fold of pieced fabric, aligning seamline with one of the marked lines at the lower edge of gourd.

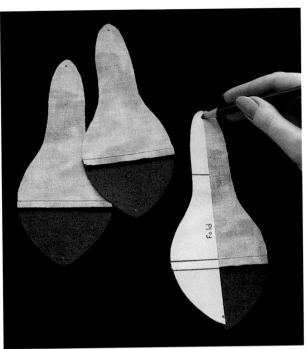

2) Lengthen or shorten neck of gourd on marked line, if desired. Cut out gourd; transfer markings to wrong side of fabric. Repeat for a total of three gourd sections.

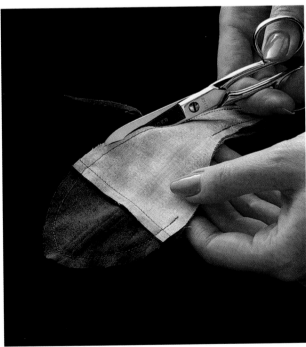

3) Pin two gourd pieces right sides together, matching dots. Stitch from top dot to bottom dot, ¼" (6 mm) from raw edges. Repeat to stitch third gourd section to first two sections. Leave about 2" (5 cm) opening on one side for turning and stuffing. Trim seam allowances ⅛" (3 mm) from stitching.

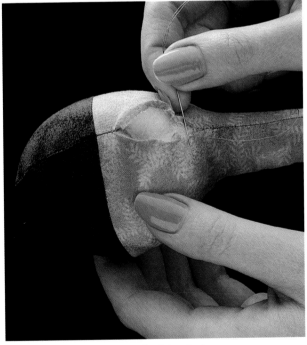

4) Cut chenille stem and whipstitch to one seam allowance as on page 80, step 14. Turn gourd right side out; stuff with polyester fiberfill, using the eraser end of a pencil. Slipstitch opening closed. Shape the neck of the gourd.

How to Make an Autumn Harvest Wall Arrangement

1) Divide 16-oz. (450 g) bundle of raffia in half; only a half bundle is needed for this project. Divide half in half again. Twist one bundle at center to make an 18" (46 cm) twisted loop; secure with rubber binder. Twist second bundle at center to make a 13" (33 cm) loop; secure with rubber binder.

2) Divide raffia tails below largest twisted loop into three bunches. Braid for about 9" (23 cm), and secure with a rubber binder. Position raffia bundle with the smallest twisted loop over braided bundle. Wrap the bundles together at top with several lengths of raffia; tie in a knot at the back.

3) Arrange four or five ears of corn and two or three gourds over raffia bundles as desired. Secure corn and gourds to braid of raffia, using a large upholstery needle and carpet thread or buttonhole twist.

5) Cut one 16" (40.5 cm) length and one 36" (91.5 cm) length from ribbon; set aside. Make several loops from remaining ribbon by folding ribbon back and forth in 8" to 10" (20.5 to 25.5 cm) lengths. Secure at center with 16" (40.5 cm) length of ribbon, and tie to raffia bundle. Tie 36" (91.5) ribbon tails around top of raffia bundle under twisted loops, and knot at back. Allow ribbon tails to dangle over arrangement.

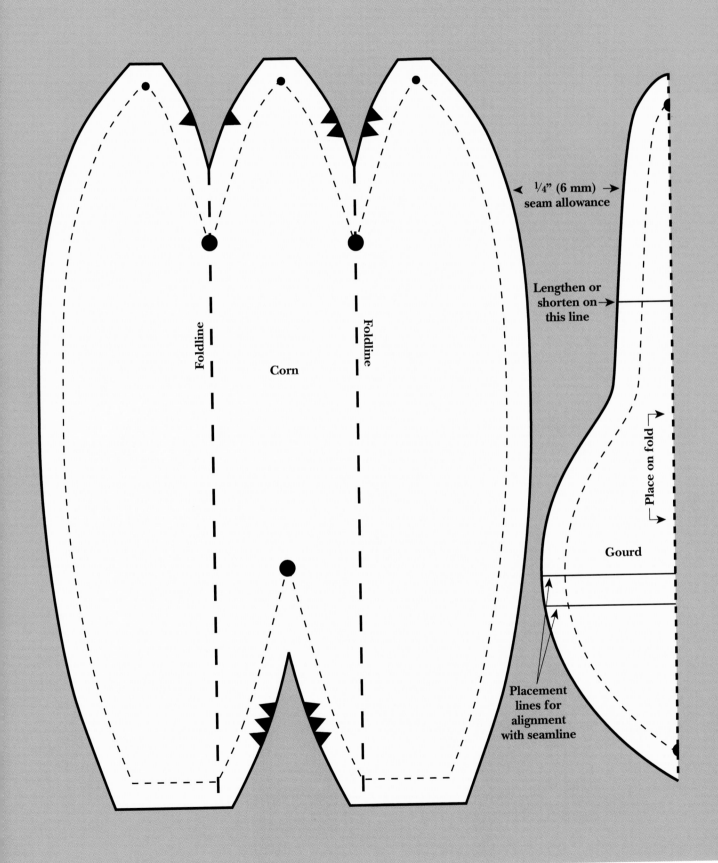

Foldline

Foldline

Corn

¼" (6 mm) → seam allowance

Lengthen or shorten on → this line

← Place on fold →

Gourd

Placement lines for alignment with seamline

Autumn Table Runners

Create a stunning quilted autumn table runner to be used throughout the season. This table runner features five basket quilt blocks, each filled with colorful appliquéd autumn leaves. The veins of the leaves are quilted, using free-motion stitching. To quilt using free-motion stitching, cover or drop the feed dogs and guide the fabric by hand in order to stitch in any direction without repositioning the fabric. It is helpful to use a darning foot for free-motion stitching. To stitch the veins in the various-colored leaves without changing thread colors, you may wish to use monofilament nylon thread.

✂ Cutting Directions

Cut one 15" (38 cm) square each from the basket background fabric and primary basket fabric. Cut one 9½" × 15" (24.3 × 38 cm) rectangle each from primary and secondary basket fabrics. Cut one 2½" (6.5 cm) strip across the width of the primary basket fabric.

From the basket background fabric, cut three 2½" (6.5 cm) strips across the width of the fabric. From these strips, cut ten 2½" × 8½" (6.5 × 21.8 cm) rectangles and ten 2½" (6.5 cm) squares. Also cut three 8⅞" (22.8 cm) squares; then cut the squares diagonally to make six triangles.

From the fabrics for the appliquéd leaves, cut 25 leaves as desired, using the patterns on page 97.

From the fabric for the background of the table runner, cut two 18¼" (46.6 cm) squares; then cut the squares diagonally in both directions to make eight triangles. Also cut two 9⅜" (24 cm) squares; then cut the squares in half diagonally to make four triangles for the corners of the table runner.

From the binding fabric, cut five 2½" (6.5 cm) strips across the width of the fabric.

From the backing fabric, cut one 21" × 89" (53.5 × 226 cm) rectangle, piecing as necessary.

YOU WILL NEED

1 yd. (0.95 m) fabric, for basket background.

⅝ yd. (0.6 m) primary basket fabric.

⅓ yd. (0.32 m) secondary basket fabric.

⅞ yd. (0.8 m) fabric, for background of table runner.

½" yd. (0.5 m) binding fabric.

¼" yd. (0.25 m) each of five fabrics, for appliquéd leaves.

Low-loft batting, about 21" × 89" (53.5 × 226 cm) rectangle.

Easy Angle II™ cutting tool.

Tear-away stabilizer.

1¼ yd. (1.15 m) fabric, for backing.

How to Sew an Autumn Table Runner

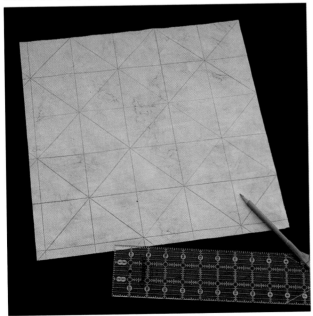

1) Draw horizontal and vertical lines on wrong side of basket background square 2⅞" (7.2 cm) apart, making a 5 × 5 grid. Draw diagonal lines through the grid as shown. There will be one diagonal line through each square.

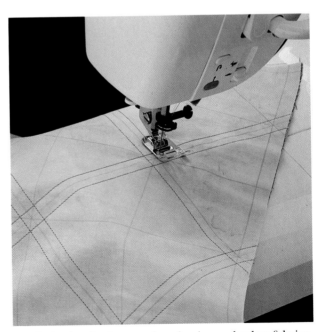

2) Pin basket background and primary basket fabrics right sides together. Stitch ¼" (6 mm) from each side of each diagonal line. Cut on all pencil lines to make triangle-squares. Press seam allowances toward basket fabric. Trim off points.

(Continued on next page)

How to Sew an Autumn Table Runner (continued)

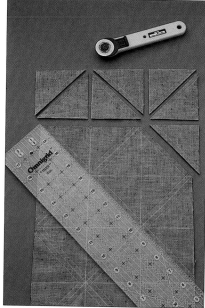

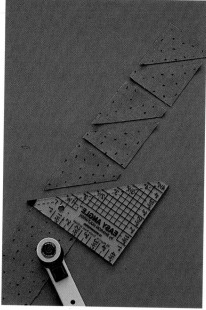

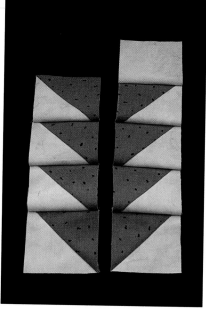

3) Draw horizontal and vertical lines on wrong side of the lightest-colored 9½" × 15" (24.3 × 38 cm) rectangle of primary or secondary basket fabric, 2⅞" (7.2 cm) apart, to make a 3 × 5 grid. Draw diagonal lines through corners of squares of grid. Continue as in step 2.

4) Align the Easy Angle II™ cutting tool with 2½" (6.5 cm) fabric strip from the primary basket fabric at the marking for the 2½" (6.5 cm) right triangle; cut along diagonal edge of tool. Continue, to make 20 triangles.

5) Stitch four triangle-squares from primary basket fabric and basket background fabric together as shown. Stitch four additional triangle-squares together, stitching a 2½" (6.5 cm) square from fabric for basket background to one end as shown.

6) Stitch short triangle-square strip to short side of large triangle from fabric for basket background as shown. Press the seam allowances away from large triangle. Stitch remaining triangle-square strip to remaining short side of large triangle; press seam allowances away from large triangle.

7) Arrange five leaves over pieced unit, extending stems of some leaves over diagonal edge of large triangle and overlapping leaves as desired. Secure leaves in place with glue stick.

8) Place tear-away stabilizer under pieced unit. Stitch ⅛" (3 mm) from raw edges of leaves, using a darning foot and free-motion stitching; use your hands to guide the fabric as you stitch. Trim any leaves extending beyond the pieced unit even with diagonal edge of large triangle.

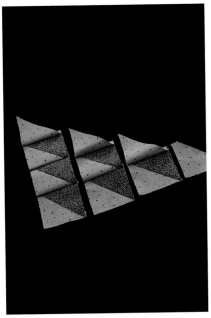

9) Stitch trangle-squares from primary and secondary basket fabrics and small triangles from secondary basket fabric into rows as shown.

10) Stitch rows together, finger-pressing the seam allowances in opposite directions. Do not press. Stitch pieced unit from basket fabrics to pieced unit with leaf appliqués as shown.

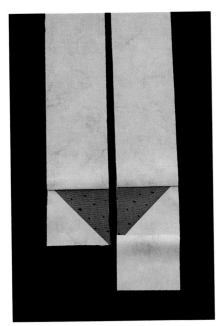

11) Stitch 2½" × 8½" (6.5 × 21.8 cm) rectangle and triangle-square from secondary basket fabric and basket background fabric together to make strip as shown. Repeat; then stitch 2½" (6.5 cm) square to triangle-square end of one strip as shown.

12) Stitch shortest strip to basket unit as shown. Stitch remaining strip to basket unit to complete basket block.

13) Stitch the triangles and pieced baskets together into rows as shown in diagram on page 97. Stitch rows together, staggering the baskets as shown in diagram, if desired.

(Continued on next page)

14) Stitch small triangle from background fabric of table runner to pieced basket at upper edge of row one. Repeat at lower edge of row five to complete pieced table runner top. Press.

15) Layer backing, batting, and table runner top; pin layers together, using safety pins spaced about 6" (15 cm) apart. Quilt by stitching in the seamlines of the blocks. Stitch veins in the leaves as desired by using free-motion stitching and a darning foot. Quilt background triangles of table runner by stitching lines 1⅛" (2.8 cm) apart along the diagonal sides of the triangles.

16) Press the binding strip in half lengthwise, wrong sides together. Pin binding strip to the right side of table runner on one long edge, matching the raw edges. Stitch ¼" (6 mm) from raw edges. Trim to scant ½" (1.3 cm).

17) Wrap the binding strip snugly around the edge of table runner, covering stitching line on back of runner; pin. Stitch in the ditch on right side of the runner, catching the binding on back side.

18) Stitch binding strip on remaining long edge as in steps 16 and 17. Stitch binding strips onto short edges as in step 16; leave ends of binding extending ½" (1.3 cm) beyond finished edges; secure the binding as in step 17, folding ends over finished edges.

Patterns for the Appliquéd Leaves of the Autumn Table Runner

Diagram of Row Assembly
for the Autumn Table Runner

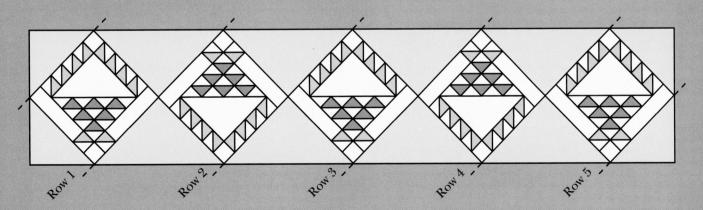

Row 1   Row 2   Row 3   Row 4   Row 5

More Projects for Thanksgiving

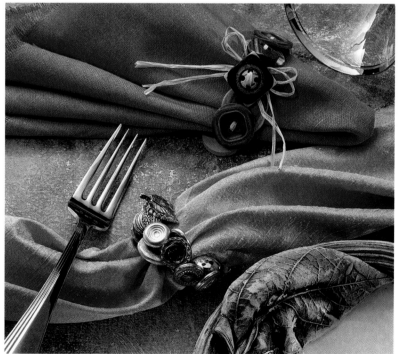

Birch wreath (above) is embellished with fabric gourds and colored corn (page 86), clustered around the top of the wreath. Wired ribbon loops are arranged around the cluster, and the ribbon tails are woven through the remainder of the wreath. Dried yarrow, safflowers, and preserved myrtle are added for a natural look.

Napkin rings (left) are created by stringing buttons together to make a 6" to 7" (15 to 18 cm) circle. The gold-tone elegant-style buttons are strung on gold metallic elastic cording. The natural-looking flat buttons are strung together on raffia. A raffia bow at the end finishes the napkin ring.

Scarecrow (above) was converted from the elf pattern (page 47) by using raffia for the hair and as accents around the pants legs and wrist areas. The scarecrow has button eyes, a chalk-marked nose, and a mouth embroidered in an outline stitch as on page 119. The ears, shoes, and the buckles on the suspenders were eliminated for the scarecrow.

Wall pockets (right) are a variation of the basket ornaments (page 17). Leather and braided raffia hangers stitched to the back of the ornaments replace the basket handle. Fill the wall pockets with miniature craft gourds, sunflowers, bittersweet, or autumn leaves.

Easter

lettuce

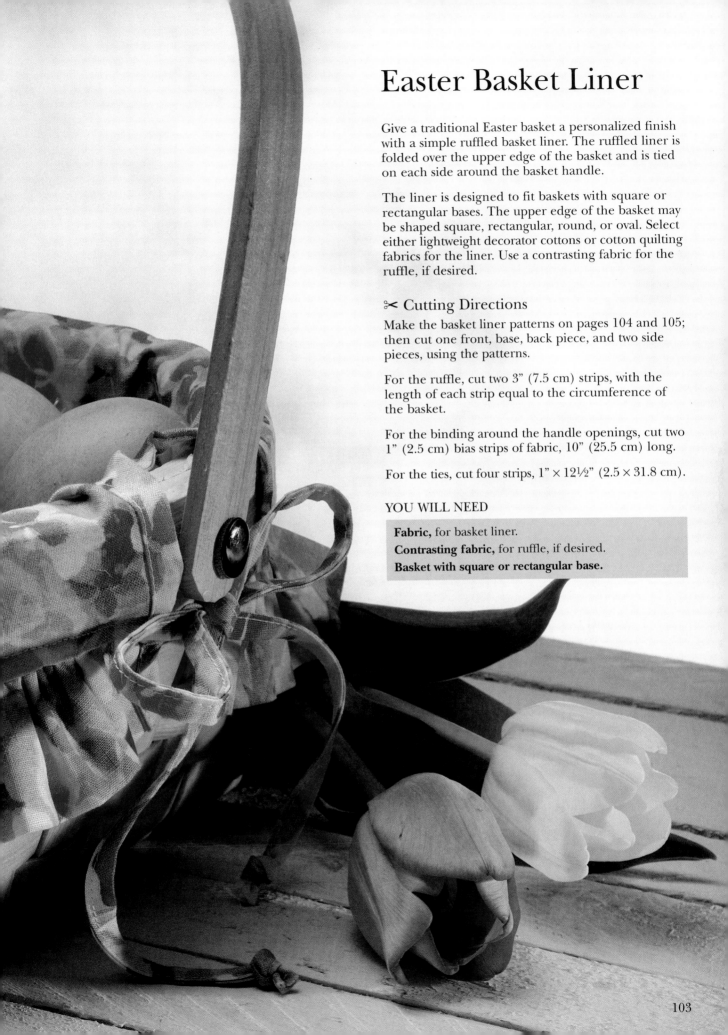

Easter Basket Liner

Give a traditional Easter basket a personalized finish with a simple ruffled basket liner. The ruffled liner is folded over the upper edge of the basket and is tied on each side around the basket handle.

The liner is designed to fit baskets with square or rectangular bases. The upper edge of the basket may be shaped square, rectangular, round, or oval. Select either lightweight decorator cottons or cotton quilting fabrics for the liner. Use a contrasting fabric for the ruffle, if desired.

✂ Cutting Directions

Make the basket liner patterns on pages 104 and 105; then cut one front, base, back piece, and two side pieces, using the patterns.

For the ruffle, cut two 3" (7.5 cm) strips, with the length of each strip equal to the circumference of the basket.

For the binding around the handle openings, cut two 1" (2.5 cm) bias strips of fabric, 10" (25.5 cm) long.

For the ties, cut four strips, 1" × 12½" (2.5 × 31.8 cm).

YOU WILL NEED

Fabric, for basket liner.
Contrasting fabric, for ruffle, if desired.
Basket with square or rectangular base.

How to Make the Pattern for the Basket Liner

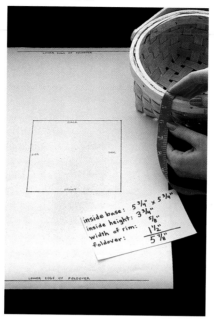

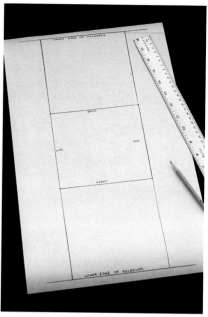

inside base: 5 3/4" × 5 3/4"

inside base: 5 3/4" × 5 3/4"
inside height: 3 3/4"
width of rim: 5/8"
foldover: 1 1/2"
5 7/8"

1) Measure the base of the basket from the inside of the basket. Draw dimensions of base on paper. Mark front, back, and sides. Mark a dot in each of the four corners.

2) Draw line parallel to and longer than front base line out a distance equal to measurement of inside height of basket plus width of rim plus desired amount for foldover on outside front of basket; repeat for back. Label marked lines as lower edge of foldover.

3) Extend lines for sides of basket base until they meet lines marked in step 2.

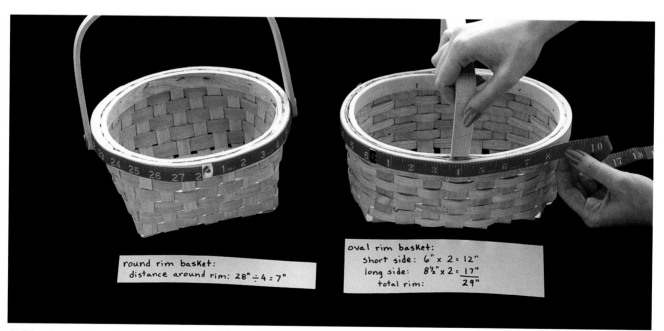

round rim basket:
distance around rim: 28" ÷ 4 = 7"

oval rim basket:
short side: 6" × 2 = 12"
long side: 8 1/2" × 2 = 17"
total rim: 29"

4) Measure distance around rim of baskets that are square or round, and divide measurement by four to get measurement around rim on each side of basket; record measurement. For baskets that are rectangular or oval, measure distance around rim on short side of basket and distance around rim on long side of basket; record measurements. For rectangular or oval baskets, twice the distance around the rim on the short side plus twice the distance around the rim of the long side should equal the total measurement around rim of basket.

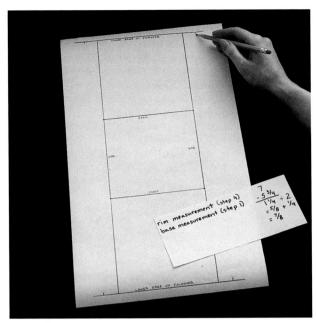

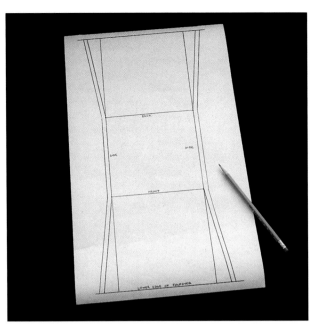

5) Take measurement around rim of front, back, and sides recorded in step 4, and subtract measurement of corresponding side of base from step 1; divide by two and add ¼" (6 mm) for ease. Mark point this distance from extended sides along lines labeled for lower edge of foldover. A negative number indicates the rim is smaller than the base. Mark a negative distance to the inside on the foldover line.

6) Draw lines connecting marked points in step 5 to points at ends of base lines as shown. Add ¼" (6 mm) seam allowance to sides as shown. This is pattern for front, back, and base of liner.

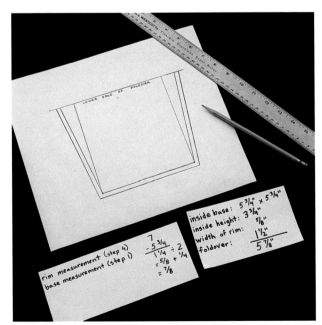

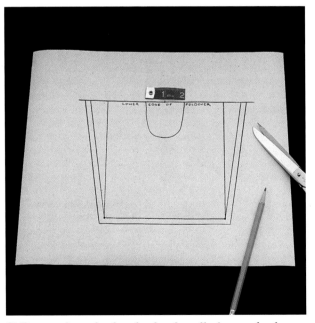

7) Draw a line the measurement of base side; mark point at each end. Repeat step 2 for base side. Draw line perpendicular to base line at each end, from the base line to line marked for lower edge of foldover. Follow steps 5 and 6 to complete pattern for sides of basket liner; in step 6, add ¼" (6 mm) seam allowances to sides and bottom of pattern.

8) Determine whether basket handle is attached to the front and back of the basket or to the sides. Mark the center of the corresponding pattern pieces along line labeled for lower edge of foldover. Mark points 1" (2.5 cm) from each side of center mark and 2" (5 cm) down from center mark. Draw semicircle connecting marks. Cut out semicircle.

How to Make a Basket Liner

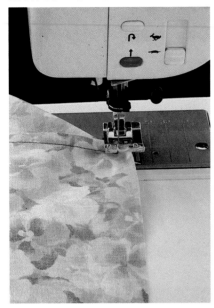

1) Transfer marked points on the pattern to fabric. Pin one side piece to the front, base, and back piece, right sides together, matching raw edges and matching points at base. Stitch ¼" (6 mm) from raw edges along side; stop at marked point at base with needle down, and pivot. Continue stitching along the base, pivoting at marked point; continue stitching remaining side.

2) Finish seam allowances with zigzag or serger stitching. Press seam allowances toward side panels. Fold ruffle strip in half, wrong sides together; press. Zigzag over cord a scant ¼" (6 mm) from raw edge. Repeat for remaining ruffle.

3) Divide ruffle strip in half; pin-mark. Pin-mark centers of upper edges of basket liner between the openings for handles. Pin ruffle piece to right side of upper edge of basket liner at center pin marks and end, matching the raw edges. Pull up gathering cord to fit; pin in place. Stitch ¼" (6 mm) from raw edges. Repeat for remaining ruffle piece.

4) Press seam allowances toward the basket liner. Topstitch on front side of the basket liner a scant ¼" (6 mm) from ruffled edge.

5) Fold one tie strip in half lengthwise, wrong sides together; press. Unfold tie strip. Fold raw edges in toward crease; press. Fold strip in half lengthwise, concealing raw edges. Edgestitch along side with double fold. Repeat for remaining ties.

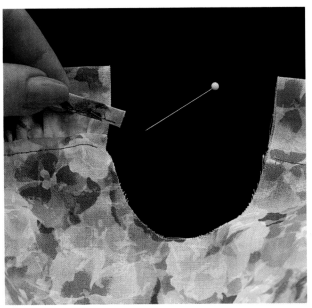

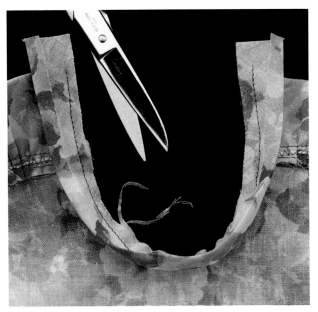

6) **Pin** tie to right side of basket liner at edge of opening for handle, aligning one long edge of tie with seamline of ruffle. Stitch in place. Repeat for remaining ties.

7) **Press** up ¼" (6 mm) to wrong side on long edge of bias binding strip. Pin the right side of remaining long edge of strip to wrong side of liner around the semicircle opening for handle; allow the short end of strip to extend ½" (1.3 cm) beyond edges of ruffles on each side. Stitch a scant ¼" (6 mm) from the raw edges; trim seam allowances.

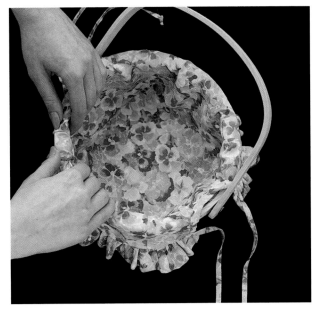

8) **Fold** ½" (1.3 cm) end of binding over finished edge; pin. Wrap long edge of binding around raw edges, and fold ties over binding; pin. Edgestitch in place close to folded edge, catching ties in stitching to hold in place. Make knot at ends of ties.

9) **Place** liner in basket, folding ruffled edge over top of basket. Tie in place around each side of handle.

Smocked Eggs

Display pretty smocked eggs in a decorative basket or hang them from an Easter tree. These eggs are smocked using checked or striped fabrics, eliminating the need to pleat the fabric in advance as with English smocking. Choose from either a smocked egg with a honeycomb pattern or a counterchange variation that combines the honeycomb design with a design that produces stripes of color between the honeycomb rows. The smocking stitches are made using three strands of embroidery floss, 2 mm silk ribbon, or pearl cotton. Use floss that matches or is slightly darker than one of the colors in the fabric.

Embellish the smocked eggs with ribbon roses or artificial leaves and flowers, available at craft and fabric stores. An optional ribbon hanger can be secured to the top of the eggs, for hanging.

✂ Cutting Directions

For each egg, cut one 6" × 16" (15 × 40.5 cm) rectangle from fabric.

YOU WILL NEED

Styrofoam® egg, about 2½" (6.5 cm) in diameter.

¼ yd. (0.25 m) fabric, such as ¼" (6 mm) gingham check or ¼" (6 mm) stripe; ¼ yd. (0.25 m) makes two smocked eggs.

Embroidery floss, 2 mm silk ribbon, or pearl cotton; needle, such as #7 darner or crewel embroidery needle.

Ribbon roses or artificial flowers and leaves, for embellishment.

Ribbon, for hanger, if desired, and for embellishment.

Tips for Smocking

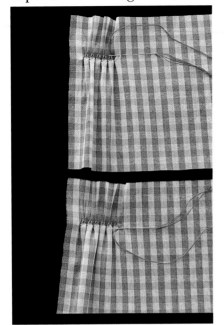

Hold thread above the needle when making stitches at the top of the row, and hold thread below the needle when making stitches at the bottom of the row.

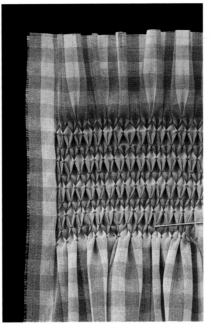

Work stitches from left to right.

Hold fabric above and below the vertical stitches while pulling floss to make pleat.

How to Smock Fabric

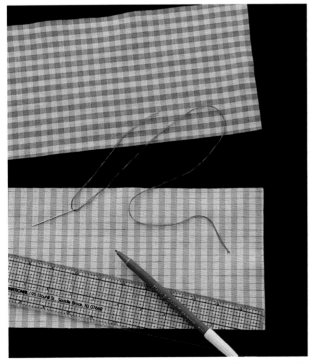

Honeycomb. 1) Thread the needle with 3 strands of embroidery floss; separate strands before threading needle, and tie together in knot at end. If using striped fabric, mark lines on fabric at ¼" (6 mm) intervals across the stripes, using water-soluble marking pen. It is not necessary to mark gingham check fabric.

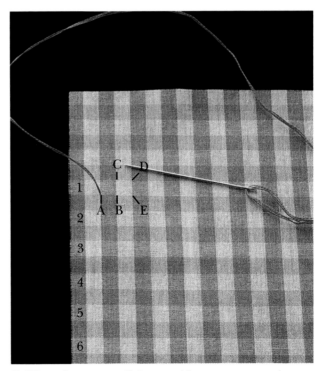

2) Plan placement of six smocking rows, centering rows on 6" (15 cm) width of fabric and allowing a plain row of fabric between each smocked row. Beginning with row one, ½" (1.3 cm) from edge of fabric, bring needle to front of fabric at Point A and pull floss through.

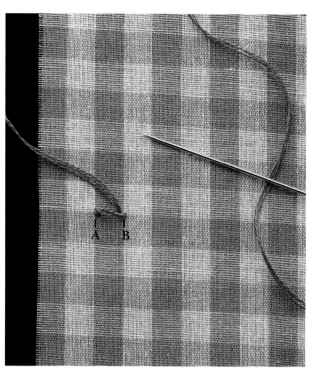

3) Insert needle to back side of fabric 3 or 4 threads to the right of Point A and back up at Point A; pull floss through.

4) Insert needle to back side of fabric at Point B and back up 3 or 4 threads to the left of Point B; pull floss through, leaving it loose so fabric lies flat.

5) Repeat step 4 at Point C; pull floss tight, drawing Points A and B together, creating first pleat.

6) Repeat step 4 at Point D. Repeat step 4 at Point E; pull floss tight, drawing Points C and D together, creating second pleat.

(Continued on next page)

How to Smock Fabric (continued)

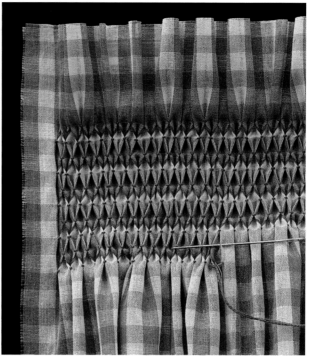

7) Continue smocking in this manner across row one, leaving floss loose on horizontal stitches and pulling it tight on vertical stitches. Tie knot in floss on back side of fabric, ½" (1.3 cm) from edge of fabric.

8) Continue to smock rows two through six as on page 110, steps 1 to 7, for smocking with a honeycomb effect.

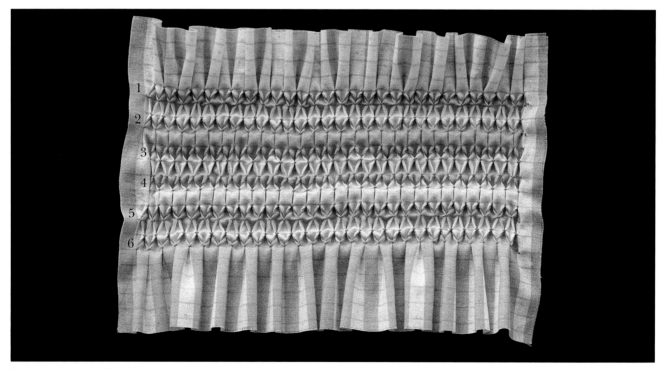

Counterchange. Smock rows in order, smocking rows one, two, five, and six as on page 110, steps 1 to 7. For rows three and four, begin smocking ¼" (6 mm) to the right of row one. Staggering the rows produces stripes of color between the honeycomb patterns.

How to Make a Smocked Egg

1) **Smock** fabric (pages 110 to 112). Center and wrap the smocked fabric around Styrofoam® egg, turning under raw edge of one short end at back of egg and overlapping short ends; pin.

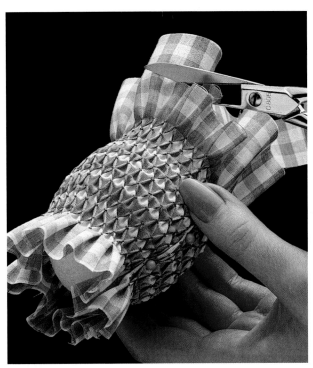

2) **Trim** off excess fabric at upper and lower edges of smocked rectangle, so raw edges just meet at top and bottom of egg.

3) **Gather** fabric close to upper and lower edges of smocked rectangle, using hand running stitches; pull up gathering threads as tight as possible. Secure in place with hand stitches; pull the raw edges together tightly with stitching. Slipstitch the overlapped ends together at back of egg.

4) **Make** hanger, if desired, from 9" (23 cm) length of ribbon; secure to top of egg with pin. To conceal raw edges of fabric, stitch ribbon roses to top and bottom of egg, or secure artificial leaves and flowers to egg, using hot glue.

Felt Rabbit

Create a clever-looking plush felt rabbit to display all year long, dressing him up with accessories for the appropriate holiday. For Easter, he carries a basket filled with colorful wooden eggs. He is dressed in a nonremovable vest and has a bow tie that can be changed as desired. For other accessories, try a pair of wire-rimmed craft glasses or a straw hat.

The rabbit has wired ears so they can be posed as desired. His face is created using craft animal eyes and embroidery floss for the nose and mouth. Cotton crochet thread is used to make the whiskers. And his tail is made from a large covered button. The finished rabbit stands about 10" (25.5 cm) tall, excluding his ears.

✂ Cutting Directions

Trace the pattern pieces as in step 1, below. Then cut two side head pieces and one center head piece from plush felt. Cut two side body pieces and two center body pieces from plush felt. Cut four arm pieces and four feet pieces from plush felt. Cut two ear pieces each from plush felt and ivory felt.

Cut one 4½" × 16½" (11.5 × 41.8 cm) rectangle for vest.

YOU WILL NEED

½ yd. (0.5 m) plush felt, for rabbit.

One square ivory felt, for inner ears.

⅛ yd. (0.15 m) felt, for vest.

Polyester fiberfill.

10 mm craft animal eyes.

Embroidery floss, for nose and mouth.

Three-cord crochet thread, size 30, for whiskers.

¼ yd. (0.25 m) elastic cord.

Ribbon, for bow tie.

Button kit, for 1½" (3.8 cm) button, to be covered for tail.

20-gauge craft wire; wire cutter.

Pink cosmetic blush.

Accessories, such as miniature basket and wooden eggs, wire-rimmed craft glasses, or small straw hat.

How to Sew a Felt Rabbit

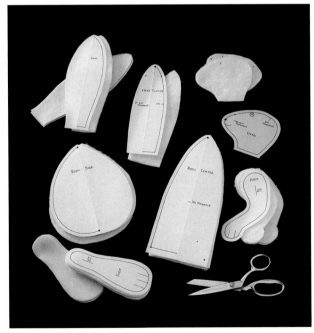

1) Trace pattern pieces (pages 120 and 121) onto paper, placing any dotted lines on the fold of the paper. Cut out patterns, adding seam allowances as indicated on patterns. Cut pattern pieces from fabric (above). Transfer markings for eyes to right side of felt and all other markings to wrong side of felt, using light pencil marks.

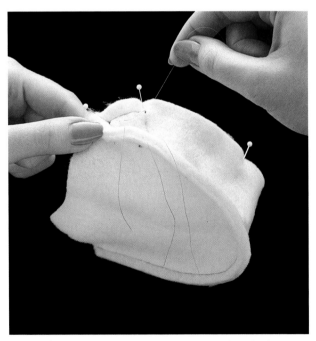

2) Stitch between small dots on center head piece. Pin center head piece to side head piece, matching dots; pull bobbin thread of stitching on center piece to ease fit. Stitch from large dot at nose to neck opening, ¼" (6 mm) from raw edges. Repeat for second side head piece.

(Continued on next page)

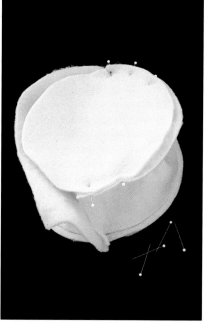

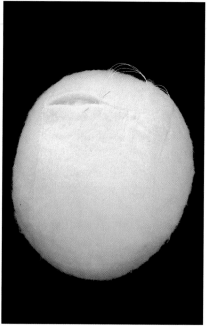

3) Stitch side head pieces together along front, from large dot to neck opening. Turn head right side out. Insert eyes at points indicated on pattern, and push disk over back to hold in place. Stuff the head with polyester fiberfill.

4) Pin one center body piece to one side body piece, from small dot at top to large dot at bottom. Stitch between dots ¼" (6 mm) from raw edges. Repeat with second center body piece. Repeat to stitch second side piece.

5) Turn body right side out. Stuff with polyester fiberfill. Slipstitch opening closed.

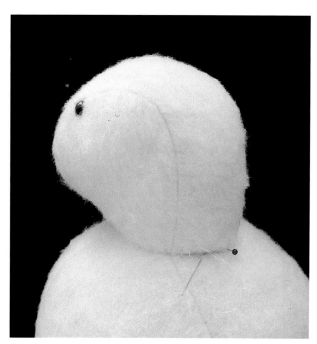

6) Turn under ¼" (6 mm) along the neck edge, and pin head to top of body as desired. Hand-stitch head to body.

7) Pin one plush ear piece to one ivory felt inner ear piece, right sides together. Stitch around ear ¼" (6 mm) from raw edges, leaving bottom open. Zigzag over craft wire, just outside previous stitching; a cording foot helps to guide wire. Cut craft wire ½" (1.3 cm) from ear opening. Repeat for remaining ear.

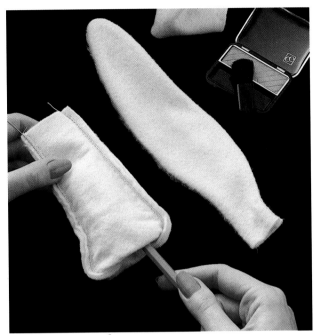

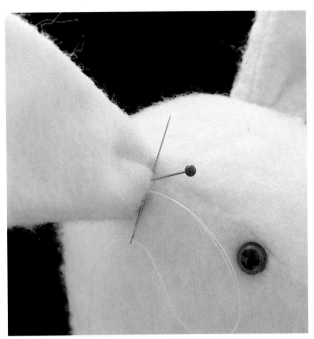

8) Turn ear right side out, using the eraser end of a pencil. Apply cosmetic blush lightly to center of ivory inner ear. Using scrap of felt, rub over center of ear to remove excess blush. Repeat for remaining ear.

9) Turn under ¼" (6 mm) at bottom of ear. Fold a small tuck at lower edge of inner ear; pin ear to head at marked points. Hand-stitch ear in place. Repeat for remaining ear.

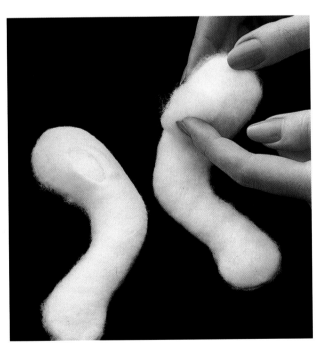

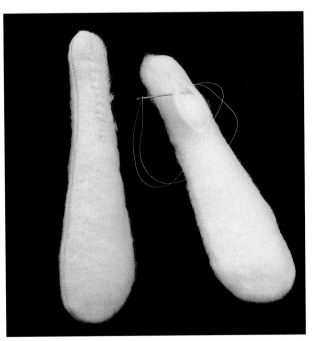

10) Make slit in one inner arm piece as indicated on pattern. Pin inner arm piece to second arm piece, right sides together. Stitch ¼" (6 mm) from raw edges. Turn right side out through slit. Lightly stuff arm with polyester fiberfill. Hand-stitch slit closed. Repeat for remaining arm, cutting slit in piece for inside of arm.

11) Make slit in two foot pieces as indicated on the pattern, for top of foot. Pin top foot piece to second foot piece, right sides together. Stitch ¼" (6 mm) from raw edges. Turn right side out through slit in top foot piece. Stuff lightly with polyester fiberfill. Hand-stitch slit closed. Repeat for remaining foot.

(Continued on next page)

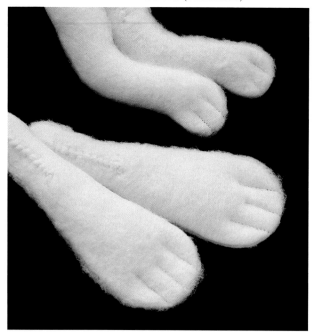

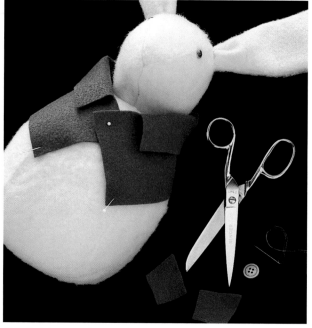

12) Stitch fingers on hands as indicated on pattern. Stitch toes on feet as indicated on pattern.

13) Fold over about 1½" (3.8 cm) on one long edge of rectangle for vest, tapering to 1¼" (3.2 cm) at ends of rectangle to make collar. Wrap vest around rabbit's neck, and overlap at center front; pin. Trim away portion of collar that overlaps at front on both sides. Secure vest layers together by stitching button at front.

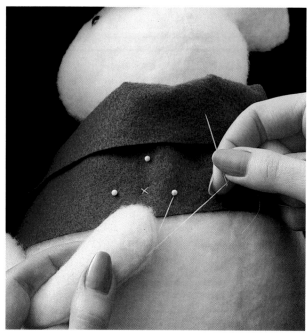

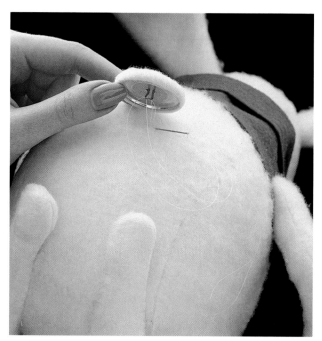

14) Mark placement for arms on vest, just below collar, about 1" (2.5 cm) from back seam, using pins. Stitch vest to body at center of marked area for arm. Hand-stitch arms to vest 1" (2.5 cm) on each side of arm center at shoulder.

15) Position feet under rabbit so rabbit is balanced; mark location. Hand-stitch feet to body at marked locations. Cover the button for tail, following the manufacturer's directions. Hand-stitch to back of rabbit at tail placement.

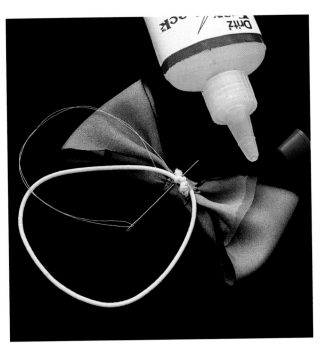

16) Make a bow from ribbon; apply liquid fray preventer to cut ends of ribbon. Secure bow with hand stitching at back. Cut elastic cording to fit around neck of rabbit plus ¾" (2 cm); tie ends of cord in knot. Hand-stitch knotted end of cording to back of bow. Place bow around neck of rabbit.

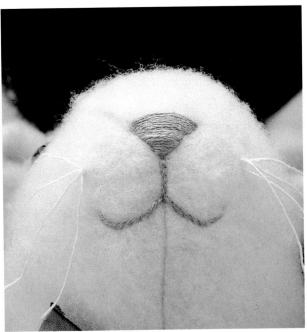

17) Embroider face as shown below. Thread needle with two lengths of cotton crochet thread. Take small stitch at marked point for whiskers; trim thread to about 3" (7.5 cm). Separate threads, and tie ends from different lengths together. Repeat on opposite side. Trim whiskers to about 1½" (3.8 cm).

How to Embroider the Facial Details

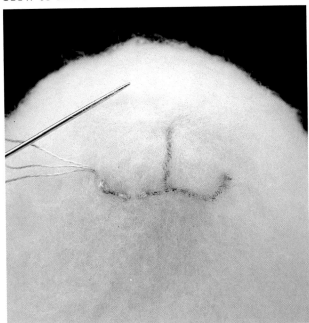

Outline stitch. 1) Mark mouth lightly with pencil. Secure threads by inserting needle along marked line, about ½" (1.3 cm) to right of starting point. Take short running stitches, as shown, until starting point is reached. Bring threaded needle through fabric from underside at starting point.

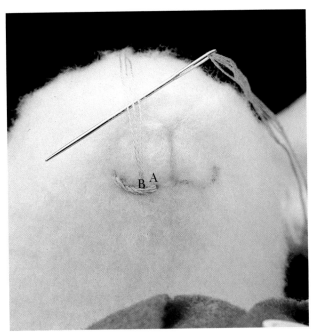

2) Take backstitches by inserting needle to underside at Point A and up a scant ⅛" (3 mm) away at Point B. Continue stitching along the marked line to end. At end, knot thread and pull knot to underside of fabric.

(Continued on next page)

How to Embroider the Facial Details (continued)

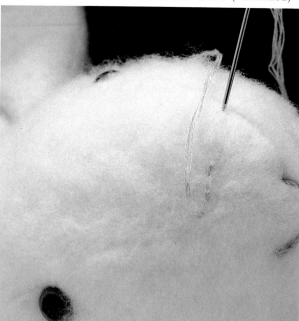

Satin Stitch. 1) Secure the threads as on page 119, step 1. Bring needle through fabric from underside at seam. Insert needle at seam directly opposite to make first stitch.

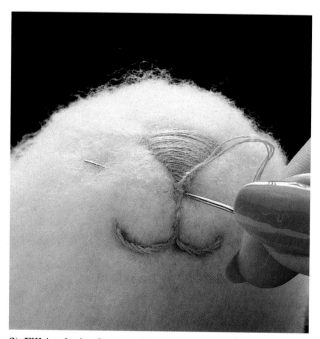

2) Fill in desired area with closely spaced parallel stitches. At end, knot thread and pull the knot to underside of fabric.

Patterns for Felt Rabbit

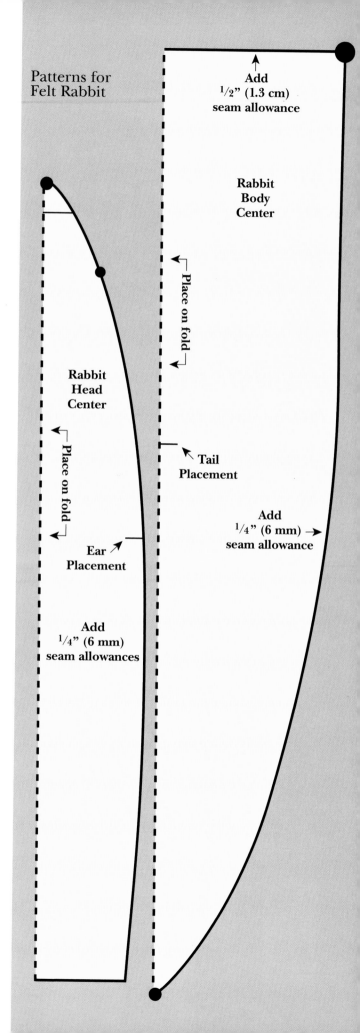

Add
$1/2$" (1.3 cm)
seam allowance

Rabbit
Body
Center

Place on fold

Rabbit
Head
Center

Place on fold

Tail
Placement

Add
$1/4$" (6 mm)
seam allowance

Ear
Placement

Add
$1/4$" (6 mm)
seam allowances

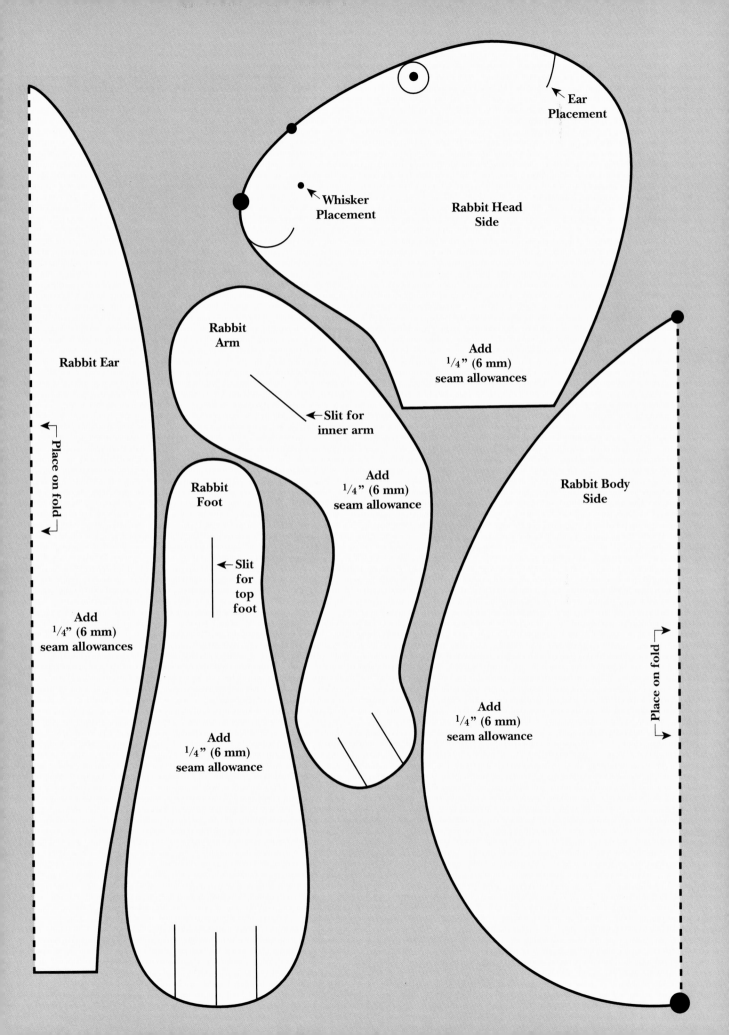

Table runner (page 93) is stitched in pastel fabrics for Easter. Eggs replace the autumn leaves. An egg-shaped cookie cutter was used for the egg pattern.

Garlands (page 30) are created from cotton quilting fabrics. Chick and butterfly designs were traced from cookie cutters. The rabbit holds a miniature carrot craft button. Seed beads are used to make the eyes on the chick and rabbit motifs. Designs are strung together on colored raffia with yo-yos and pastel buttons.

122

More Projects
for Easter

Easter card (right) features a pot full of spring flowers. Flower heads and pot are padded and hand-stitched to card as on page 63. Stems are stitched using embroidery floss and outline stitches.

Tree (below) is painted a soft yellow and embellished with fabric-wrapped eggs. Wrap Styrofoam® eggs as on page 31, step 1. Make the hanger from narrow ribbon.

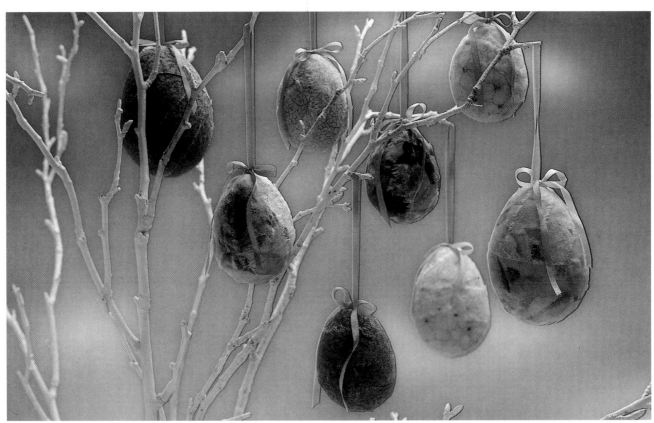

Projects for Other Holidays

Independence Day wall hanging (left) is made using the basic instructions for the Halloween wall hanging (page 69). Four printed fabric blocks are substituted for the four appliquéd blocks. The wall hanging is hung from a branch. Padded star cookie-cutter shapes, made as on page 32, hang from the ends of the branch.

St. Patrick's Day leprechaun (below) is a variation of the Christmas elf (page 39). The leprechaun is dressed in green and is wearing a craft felt top hat. Craft doll buckles decorate his shoes.

Basket liner (page 103) is used for an Independence Day picnic basket.

May Day basket (right) is created from the basket ornament (page 17). The basket is filled with pastel mints.

Valentine's Day card is made from a collage of pink and metallic fabrics and tulle. A heart charm and beads are secured to the front of the card. Make the card as on page 65.

Index

Cowles Creative Publishing, Inc.
offers a variety of how-to books. For
information write:
  Cowles Creative Publishing
  Subscriber Books
  5900 Green Oak Drive
  Minnetonka, MN 55343